'All-to-One'
The Winning Model for Marketing
in the Post-Internet Economy

'All-to-One'

The Winning Model
for Marketing in the
Post-Internet Economy

Steve Luengo-Jones

The McGraw-Hill Companies

London • Burr Ridge, IL • New York • St Louis • San
Francisco • Auckland • Bogotá • Caracas • Lisbon • Madrid
Mexico • Milan • Montreal • New Delhi • Panama • Paris
San Juan • São Paulo • Singapore • Tokyo • Toronto

Published by
McGraw-Hill Publishing Company
SHOPPENHANGERS ROAD, MAIDENHEAD, BERKSHIRE, SL6 2QL, ENGLAND
Telephone: +44(0) 1628 502500
Fax: +44(0) 1628 770224
Web site: http://www.mcgraw-hill.co.uk

British Library Cataloguing in Publication Data
A catalogue record for this book is available from the British Library

-

ISBN 0 07 709799 8

Library of Congress Cataloguing-in-Publication Data
The LOC data for this book has been applied for and may be obtained from
the Library of Congress, Washington, D.C.

Author's Web site address: http://www.all-to-one.com

Sponsoring Editor: Elizabeth Robinson
Produced by: Steven Gardiner Ltd
Cover: Simon Levy
Page design: Mike Cotterell
Typesetting: Mouse Nous, Cross-in-Hand

The McGraw·Hill Companies

While every precaution has been taken in the preparation of this book,
neither the authors, nor McGraw-Hill, shall have any liability with respect
to any loss or damage caused directly or indirectly by the instructions or
advice contained in the book.

Printed in Great Britain by Bell and Bain Ltd., Glasgow

1   2   3   4   5   CUP   5   4   3   2   1

To the memory of my father
Raymond Edward Jones

Contents

Acknowledgements

I HAVE TO GO back to my father Raymond Jones and my mother Margaret who have both given their wisdom in different ways. My father was always getting me to 'think different, think wide, think deep, think hard and don't be afraid of risks' (so that's where my drive for innovation comes from). My mother Margaret has always provided the bedrock, the 'keeping both feet on the ground' and the safe fall-back that encourages people to take risks. I have to thank both my parents for this firmly based balance. It's because of it that I've been able to do the things I've done. I shall not forget and will always be grateful.

That advice should go for everyone running an organisation: challenge people to innovate, take risks, try to be the best – and provide them with a safety net. That's how you make winners.

I would like to acknowledge others who have had a profound and personal effect on me. They include Gary Duggan, Wyn Hughes, Grenville Evans, Huw and Delyth Morgan (and all the Aber Cardiff Crew), Mark and Angela McGuinley, Lee Cable, John Hemming and, of course, Martin and Marian Forrest.

In my career I learnt so much from so many people (I'm still learning – it continues to be a great apprenticeship). It's difficult to pick out individuals, but some have had a profound effect: Alan Jones gave me my first chance; John Sykes, back in my Thorn EMI days, taught me the value of creating a 'family at work', a balanced team where each individual is different and has value to give (John, Pat, Rita, Michelle and Tracy, I still miss you).

At British Airways it was Jill Parker, Luke Mayhew and peers such as Wendi Pasco, Charles Weiser and many others. Jill was of particular help and guidance in a very formative stage of my career. It was a very special time for all the team. The merging of marketing, technology, people, culture and innovation provided key lessons. Time flies on and the spirit and togetherness at Avis with people such as Keith Dyer and Bruce Tranter hold great memories and experience, all utilised in this book.

More recently at EDS I value my time with Sean Finnan, Alan Hammersmith and Nadine Eddison who gave free rein to follow vision, chase innovation and be creative; with Simon Burn who has given bedrock support, unflinching in the sea of cultural change and storm; with Matt Studholme who truly understands the 'All-to-One' spirit, the hard work, risk-taking and innovation needed to achieve it; and, of course, with all the Consumer Focus team almost too numerous to mention – Lou, Leigh, Linda, Karl, Mike, Gini, Amy, James, Ulla, Jay, Wolfgang, Sam, Brenda and Brian.

A special mention to one client who shares the same evangelistic fervour, dedication and tenacity to make 'All-to-One' happen – Rob Malyn of General Motors Europe who over many, many hours of passionate discussion has helped me to hone my thoughts contained in this book. Thank you Rob and good speed in your quest. I would also like to thank Dr Wolfgang Reinhardt of Onstar Europe for his encouragement, team-building philosophies, support and strategic insight as well as the pioneering spirit – all so evident and enjoyable over the last few months.

To me the book is a summation of the things I've learnt and the experience I've gained in trying to handle all the factors involved in 'All-to-One'. The learning was done the hard way, the experience gained in real-life confrontation with real-life issues. My apprenticeship has continued with the making of this book. Putting my thoughts down on paper has helped crystallise them.

But the book, like anything worthwhile, is not a one-man creation. Putting it together has been a truly 'All-to-One' experience, with a great team.

I first have to thank Chris Thomas without whom there would have been no book. I have wanted to write it for some years and his encouragement and support have been key to making it happen.

I have to thank the wonderful Bryan Oakes to whom I will be eternally grateful. Bryan has done such a great job in pulling everything together for me, the many case studies, the examples, the quotations we have sought out together, the working on the text day in and day out, the long discussions, the generation of fire and excitement as the thing gradually came together. All these, with the hours, days, weekends of dedication, have been crucial in getting the work done in what I am told by Elizabeth Robinson, our excellent, ever-helpful and ever-encouraging editor at McGraw-Hill, has been staggeringly quick time. I am not sure who has been more enthusiastic Bryan or I – many thanks Bryan.

Jill Parker and Wendi Pasco contributed hugely to the chapters on the RelModel and on company culture. Jill, Wendi, you already have my thanks, but here they are again. Our book reviewers, commentators, and specialist contributors have all worked with us in typical 'All-to-One' spirit – among them: Chris Owens who gave us some great 'buying a car' insights as well as an illuminating case study; Karl Davies with some important input on data architecture; Matt Studholme for valuable suggestions and overview on the Enterprise Architecture chapter; Derek Kaufman with highly relevant expertise and examples from the USA; Rob Dransfield of Nottingham Trent University who provided sure guidance from his academic and business background; John Caswell who has once again provided inspiration and superb vision with an 'All-to-One' Journey Map; Mario Hytten for some incisive comments and additions; James Garcia-Luengo (yes, he's my brother-in-law) for acting as one of our reviewers; Roy Sheppard who gave sharp advice in the early stages of the book; David Cheek added key thoughts; Mike and Joanne Eldridge have been endlessly encouraging – Joanne actually read the whole text one weekend and helped critically in getting it to its final shape; and, of course, my wife Sue who can now hopefully get back to a normal life.

I intend this book to be the start of an on-going process of development and dialogue. We can continue with both on the 'All-to-One' website. I look forward to meeting you there.

Introduction

I HAVE WRITTEN this book because I believe passionately that marketing is primarily about life and the way that products and services can enhance the way people live, not primarily about anything else, and certainly not primarily about technology, electronic or otherwise, and I want to share that belief with as many people as possible. The focus must always be on people, on consumers. I believe that consumers will lead the way to profitability – if you are ready to follow. This is the marketing vision that I have followed and continue to follow and this is the vision I have tried to portray in the pages that follow.

I've also been provoked into writing the book by the way that some companies have squandered their inheritance and failed their stakeholders. We've all seen examples of this (Boo.com *et al.*). I've seen too many and I want to see no more. I hope this book will remind people that marketing is not a game, an ego trip, or a mystery best left untouched, but a simple straightforward series of techniques that anyone can apply if they have the dedication, the support and the imagination. It can be simple and I hope I can clear some space for that simplicity.

I confess too that I am irritated by the excessive claims of the Internet cheerleaders. No one is a bigger Internet enthusiast than I am. What a fantastic medium! What a gift! And we have only just begun to realise its possibilities! But the Internet has to be put into perspective, into the consumer's perspective. If anyone is tempted to be taken in by the hype, I hope I can put them right and steer them back to the consumer. In short, I want to show how consumer focus can be achieved in the post-Internet economy, the Internet-plus economy.

So, the book is based on hard practical personal experience and fiercely held beliefs. My blood and sweat lie just beneath the surface of every page. I draw on all my time in the various blue-chip, innovative and ground-breaking organisations I have worked in and for. During the late 1980s, we developed British Airways' highly successful 'loyalty' crusades, which brought together all aspects of the marketing mix to create a unique competitive advantage. We deployed the necessary tools and techniques, including world-class branding, to manage comprehensive cultural and organisational changes. The result, among much else, was a consumer-focused and caring work force, all dedicated to the unified cause of product excellence and consumer service – and who were thus able to move all the necessary mountains. At Avis, we linked the world-famous 'We try harder' culture to a new passion for innovation, to a worldwide distribution capability and to a technical infrastructure, which together created a competitive advantage rooted in consistent, first-class service for consumers. I initiated and implemented similar initiatives elsewhere before moving on to found the Consumer Focus Group at EDS.

I have a range of readers in mind for the book. Company leaders, whatever their title, will find in it a strategic view of the way the Internet can really work to its best potential and be better able to assess the true effectiveness of their company's relationships with consumers. In particular, marketing executives who want their companies to succeed in the real world will find it full of practical advice, all based on hard practical experience. And, of course, any student of marketing can treat it as an extremely accessible guide to what's really what in marketing today (and tomorrow).

In any sense, all those are the obvious target readers, and absolutely essential. But I have in mind a wider readership too. One of the downsides of the electronic revolution is its encouragement of exclusiveness. Unless checked, it tends to treat each individual as an island of specialisation with independent silos of expertise, cut off, except electronically, from the rest – 'you do that job, I do this job, she is an Internet specialist, he is not, you're in marketing they are not'. But the best marketing in the best companies happens when everyone in the company sees her or his job as a marketing job, when information and experiences can be accessed by everyone, where consumer relations are everyone's concern, in short when 'All-to-One' is everyone's motto. So you've guessed ... I'd like the book to be at least looked at and talked about by everyone in the organisation. I want people, *all* the people in every part of the organisation, to remain in control, and machines, electronic or otherwise, to remain as servants, each knowing their place and staying well within it.

At the book's heart are the chapters on the RelModel and its practical application. 'Rel' is short for relationship, and 'relationship' is the key word, the basis of all selling – which is why consumer relationship marketing (CRM) has played such an important role over the past few years. But 'All-to-One' and the RelModel take off from that CRM base to provide a new paradigm that is more effective, better workable and productive of richer rewards for the enterprise.

Incidentally, the 'C' in CRM is usually taken to stand for 'customer'. For practical purposes, I find it useful to take is as referring to 'consumer'. It's a broader term. By 'consumer' I mean several different people: (a) someone who buys your kind of product or service and is either a customer of yours or of a competitor; (b) someone who uses your kind of product but it's bought for them by someone else either from you or from a competitor; (c) someone who is a potential/likely new consumer. 'Consumers' are the total potential market. Your customers are your share of the market. The task is to turn consumers into your customers. So the prime overall target is 'consumers' which is why for the rest of this book, I shall use the word 'consumer' and mean it to include the word 'customer' too.

The RelModel chapters are buttressed by a very practical, how-to-do-it section on 'Getting closer to the consumer with RelTechnics'. I have used RelTechnics for several years now in some very tough markets. They work. I've also included a variety of case studies from a very wide range of businesses on both sides of the Atlantic and from the Pacific Rim that illustrate in their different ways how 'All-to-One' works in the real world.

So the book is intended as a practical aid as well as, I hope, an inspirational counter to the present dominance of the Internet-is-everything brigade. This is one reason why I have included a detailed and comprehensive chapter on the actual range of media we have at our disposal. It should act as a new pair of spectacles for the short-sighted Internetters, giving them a view of media riches and the richness of consumer connectivity that they appear not to see. I've tried to bring out the good things about all the media. The only thing I kick is hype – which is why I continue to kick the cult of the Internet – and I hope this book will help everyone who reads it to kick the habit too.

But because the Internet is still new and so very important, I have given a whole chapter to its best use with the help of RelWeb (Chapter 6). And I have devoted a whole chapter (Chapter 10) to internal company organisation. 'All-to-One' won't work unless the enterprise architecture is right.

These chapters are interspersed with special sections illustrating aspects of 'All-to-One'. These sections include: 'A vision of what might be'; 'The on-going technological revolution'; and 'The importance of professional accreditation'. I end with a postscript entitled: 'The 'All-to-One' future' – where we might be in 10 years' time'.

There have been many good books written over the past few years on the digital revolution, its impact, its potential and how to harness it. I provide brief reviews of some of the most noteworthy.

So far as the Internet fanatics are concerned, I suppose it's in my own narrow interests, and those of my clients, to keep quiet and let them continue to plough an electronic desert. But it pains me to think of the money that is going to be poured, that *is* being poured, into this sterile, unconnected environment, money which could be far better spent enriching the lives of the buying public and the coffers of our clients.

I believe that the message of 'All-to-One' is and will continue to be successful because its message speaks to human needs and aspirations. Nothing and no one is left out.

Book titles are often a problem. Not this one. 'All-to-One' is what it's about. 'Post-Internet' is where we are now and the new Internet-plus economy will be for some time to come. We can't de-invent the Internet, I'm glad to say. Nor, I'm even gladder to say, can we re-invent the hype that has surrounded it for too long. The hype has had its day. We are now in the 'post-Internet-hype' era, which I've shortened to 'post-Internet' – leaving out the hype. The Internet is now 'normal'. Tranquillity and common sense are being restored. We can get down at last to some full-blooded marketing, making the very most of what the Internet has to offer as we make the very most of what all the other media and marketing tools at our disposal have to offer. And I hope no one will misunderstand me when I include 'people' among those marketing tools. In an 'All-to-One' world, people are by far the most important part of the 'All'.

I hope you enjoy the book. Even more, I hope you implement it. Then we'll all benefit.

One

The 'One-to-One' Future is ... 'All-to-One'

'The old economy was about massive size, stability and quantity. The new economy is about speed, agility and quality.'

Don Uzzi, Senior Vice President of Global Marketing
Communications and Government Affairs, EDS

T HERE'S NOTHING NEW about 'one-to-one', even if you spell it 1:1. Treating people on that basis has been the hallmark of human relations ever since Adam and Eve first got together. Commercial relations too. Neolithic barterers, Viking traders (that's what they called themselves), Genoese merchants, Eastern bazaar wallahs, Wild West horse doctors, Victorian haberdashers and open-all-hours momma/poppa shop-keepers have done good business for millennia and made many friends into the bargain by treating consumers as people, one at a time, and getting as much business as possible from each one of them. The genius of Don Pepper and Martha Rogers all those eight years ago – at the time of writing – was to take that familiar age-old one-to-one concept and connect it to a brand-new, one-to-one medium – the Internet.

The connection was magic. At a stroke, it broke a myriad moulds. It shattered the belief that 'more of the same is the one business aim', a belief made possible by the mass-production techniques introduced by the Industrial Revolution 200 years ago and implemented since then by virtually every manufacturer and virtually every member of every sales force. Thanks to the one-to-one/Internet connection, the market of the masses could be replaced with the market of individuals. Loud-hailers were downgraded in favour of hand-shakers. Spray guns were beaten into snipers' rifles – firing only virtual bullets you understand. 'Buy what we tell you to buy' became 'let's talk'. Marketers were reminded that no two people are the same and that different people should be treated differently. Consumers were thrilled by the promise of new kinds of personal, bespoke buying relationships. And the unlimited possibilities of the electronic revolution and its most dynamic manifestation to date, the Internet, were revealed for all to see. (Notice how easy it is to get carried away.)

But now the world has moved on and Internet-fever has started to cool (short-lived, wasn't it?). The new economy, the Internet-plus economy, enlarged and enhanced rather than transformed by the Internet, has arrived. And the novelty has gone from 'one-to-one', at least from 'one-to-one' in its blinkered Internet-only packaging. Its one-track inadequacies are showing.

So, as the dust settles, the old truths emerge, unchanged and unavoidable. People are not content with one-track relationships with anyone including suppliers. They look for total commitment and total service, as they always have done. The product, the wrapping, the way the product is delivered, the voice at the call centre, the press and TV advertising, the website, the point-of-sale material, the posters and printed literature, the people in the store, the sales people, the service people who call round, everyone and everything must be committed and seen to be committed to each individual consumer. The supplier who does all that the best will get the sale, the loyalty, the future. The fragmented, specialist approach will always be beaten by the holistic. 'One-to-one', Internet-only, is not holistic.

So, what next?

We need a fresh vision of the old truths, a different paradigm of the old patterns, a new model of the old ways. We need 'All-to-One'.

'All-to-One' is a short-hand way of summing up a complex but inescapable commercial truth:

'individual consumers respond best, buy more and stay loyal when they feel that everyone and everything in the supplier company is committed to meeting their needs, solving their problems, and sharing their aspirations ... and they are happiest and most convinced when they are reminded of that commitment in a variety of ways in the full range of communication media.'

Or to put it another way ...

'successful long-term consumer relationships thrive on a totality of communication – personal and printed as well as electronic. And the communication must be between, on the one hand, everyone concerned in any way with manufacturing, distribution and selling the product and, on the other, the consumer who wants to buy it.'

Or to sum it all up:

'consumers prefer to be treated as people.'

'All-to-One' answers all those requirements, however expressed, in full and with flair. It is the new model for consumer relationship marketing (CRM). Through its specialist methodologies – RelModel, RelTechnics and RelWeb – it can offer the companies who implement it a *lasting* competitive advantage. The brightest and best of the blue-chips are already moving towards it. Many smaller companies have been doing it very successfully for decades without calling it 'All-to-One'. I give examples throughout the book. But 'All-to-One' is right for any kind and size of business, not excepting e-business. It is the nearest thing that business has to a natural law. Companies ignore it at their peril.

I should emphasise here that we are talking about an evolution – from where you are now to the 'All-to-One' position where lifetime value for consumer and company is maximised.

The relevance of 'All-to-One'

'All-to-One' is relevant whichever way you look at it. It is as relevant to the way a company relates to its staff and their families as to the

Production went 1:1 too

There was something else, something that made the 1:1 concept work *in today's world. That something else was a near incredible advance, a step-change, in production capability. The digital technologies that sired the Internet have also sired a new breed of manufacturing techniques. They enable companies to combine mass production economy with bespoke variety. Henry Ford Senior offered consumers the Model T in any colour they liked so long as it was black. His descendants today hardly produce the same car twice. Colour, engine size, everything else you can think of, are variable at the command of the consumer, whichever model is chosen. The time will come, and pretty quickly too, when every Ford can be tailor-built to suit a particular person. Savile Row will then have come to Detroit for keeps and potentially to every other manufacturing site in the world.*

way it relates to its consumers and prospects, and to its suppliers … it is relevant to the way it relates to the local community and to society as whole … it is relevant to the way it talks to local and national media, to local and national government officials. Companies, like people, might present different aspects of themselves in different circumstances, but each of those aspects must clearly be seen to be an aspect of the same company, the same personality.

This emphasis on consistency makes 'All-to-One' the most powerful means available to a company for creating an attractive and influential image for itself. It provides the connectivity between the company persona and its reality, the reality as experienced by the consumer. When *everything* a company does, online and offline – and in the vast majority of cases, offline – then consumers respond. You hear, or would hear if you researched it, remarks like:

'You know where you are with them.'

'They can always be relied on.'

'I bought it from them so it's sure to be good.'

'They'll always come up with the answer.'

'Whichever of their shops you go in, it's always clean and friendly.'

'The staff are always so helpful.'

These, and similar comments, are the rewards of an 'All-to-One' approach to business and contribute powerfully to the creation and maintenance of a good company image.

That's how 'All-to-One' works at the company level. It works with equal power at the brand level. 'All-to-One' works wonders with brands. Every great brand you can think of has been handled, consciously or simply by instinct, on 'All-to-One' principles. For a brand, 'All-to-One' requires everything about it to be consistently consumer-oriented – its performance, ideally its technical superiority, its name, packaging, advertising, merchandising, overall marketing. Not just everything but, as with the company's 'All-to-One' approach, every*one*. A brand has a sort of moral contract with the consumer, a promise that it will always deliver everything that's expected of it. We want the consumer to think and feel that 'this is my product, it will never let me down ... and the people who make it, deliver it, sell it, whatever, are my people, and they will never let me down.'

I remember an elderly and rather nervous friend of a friend who came to London for the first time on her own, and felt lost and lonely until she happened to pass the offices of *The Lady* magazine in Covent Garden in the centre of London, She laughs at herself now when she tells the story, but insists that when she saw the offices where her favourite magazine was published, she felt just as if she'd met an old friend among all the strangers. 'An old friend among strangers' is what every great brand is. That's what 'All-to-One' does at the brand level. I treat this highly relevant aspect more fully in Chapter 8, 'Image rules ... brand stays king'.

For me, 'All-to-One' is *the* great marketing battle cry, eminently playable on a trumpet (the acid test for any really influential concept), and as essential today as it always has been. It is comprehensive, firmly rooted in human behaviour and therefore future-proof. It is as practical and usable today as it has always been through all the centuries of buying and selling. The media through which the transactions are done do change. And, of course, the products change, though nothing like as much as the media change. Food is food, transport is transport, finery is finery whatever the century and whatever the gloss given by the branding.

The 'All-to-One' methodology covers people, systems and media, all are important, but none more so than people. 'All-to-One' is about people, and very much about the people in your company, and how to motivate and energise *everyone*, into the 'All-to-One' frame of mind. Nothing is more dispiriting than a company culture that limits consumer responsibility to people whose job descriptions contain those words.

Some of the case studies I give in the book, not all, demonstrate an aspect of the 'All-to-One' thesis that I cannot stress too strongly. It is this, and I'll put in bold type to emphasise its importance:

'All-to-One' cannot work, and the company trying to make it work cannot succeed, unless the whole of that company's organisation has been restructured to focus on the 'All-to-One' ideal.

What those words mean is really very obvious, but I'll spell the meaning out: all the company, everyone and everything in it, has to be consumer-oriented, consumer-facing – each consumer should feel that everyone (and everything) in the company is on his/her side, dedicated to providing the goods and services that he/she needs or wants, or didn't realise was needed or wanted until the 'All-to-One' company produced one and presented it.

In practice an 'All-to-One' company is a *balanced* company and all the teams within it are balanced too, balanced in a new consumer-facing way. Instead of the balance of responsibility for the consumer being weighed down to the sales force, the balance is adjusted to give everyone responsibility. The sense of commitment to the consumer has to become part of everyone's psyche and as such is intangible, but has endless tangible expressions. Here is one of them:

> Make sure that in future all information about the consumer held by the company is available to all the people in the company.

'What!' I can hear someone say, 'even the manufacturing people on the shop floor?' The answer is a resounding yes. Of course they will not make use of it in the same way as the sales people do. They will not access it with anything like the regularity of the sales people. They may not access it at all. But they can if they like. And internal publicity continually reminds them that they are as important to consumer satisfaction (on which their jobs depend) as the sales force, the directors or anyone else is, and therefore are as entitled to the same information and insights about the company and its consumers as anyone else.

This sharing of responsibility is part of the 'emotional bonding' that makes 'All-to-One' work and the company successful. In the armed forces, it used to be called 'esprit de corps' and people were prepared to die for it. In sport, it is called 'team spirit', and in good teams, players are prepared to give their all for it. Unless you achieve that in your company, that sound you hear is of the curtain starting to fall.

Balanced teams in a balanced organisation are the absolutely essential requirements for an 'All-to-One' success.

'All-to-One' means all the staff in this Brazilian family company

WHEN SEMCO, the Brazilian manufacturer of marine pumps, industrial dishwashers and mixing equipment, teetered on the edge of bankruptcy 20 years ago, its young owner Ricardo Semler introduced a particularly dramatic version of what we now know as the 'All-to-One' approach to business. He told his management and staff to disregard all the written procedures and manuals which had hitherto misguided them and to join with him in making the strategic and operational decisions. The staff had all the power and authority. They could come and go as they pleased, set their own production timetables, put major decisions to the vote, set their own salaries and bonuses and generally take over their own working lives. Company books were open to all employees. After 10 years, during which time Brazil passed through a severe recession, Semco had been transformed. The company was growing, with profits of 10 per cent on sales of £37 million.

The Semler achievement is an outstanding example of the successful working of an 'All-to-One' culture. Very few companies could take the idea to these extremes, but the principle of empowerment of everyone in the company, which lies at the heart of the 'All-to-One' approach, is here wonderfully vindicated.

Two

'All-to-One' via the RelModel

T HE 'ALL-TO-ONE' IDEAL is attainable by any size and kind of company. The RelModel methodology shows you how. It guides you through a series of levels, each of them well defined, each of them representing a level of maturity. By 'maturity' I mean a state in which the principles and procedures of each level have become integral to your company and everyone and everything in it.

As you move up, your people, structures and culture (the 'All') develop closer, more mature and ever-more productive relationships with each consumer (the 'One'). At Level 5, the final level, you have achieved the 'All-to-One' ideal, a mature relationship that delivers lifetime value to both the consumer and to your company.

Let me first give you an overview of the RelModel (I give the total picture in Chapter 3).

Overview

The RelModel (short for relationship model) is a method of maximising consumer relationships in a controlled manner. It works because it shows how to gain capability and competitive advantage cumulatively through increasing knowledge of the consumer – and then turning your competitive advantage into profit.

RelModel identifies five levels of competitive advantage which organisations can develop through consumer knowledge. Those that

The RelModel in outline

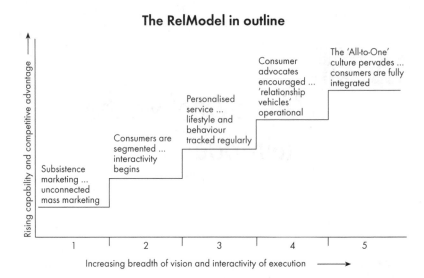

Rising capability and competitive advantage →

Subsistence marketing ... unconnected mass marketing

Consumers are segmented ... interactivity begins

Personalised service ... lifestyle and behaviour tracked regularly

Consumer advocates encouraged ... 'relationship vehicles' operational

The 'All-to-One' culture pervades ... consumers are fully integrated

1   2   3   4   5

Increasing breadth of vision and interactivity of execution ⟶

use each stage as a learning process to get closer to consumers and learn more about them, will find that they can move on to the next level more quickly.

The figure above demonstrates the process graphically.

❏ RelModel Level 1 consists of subsistence marketing, unsophisticated broadcast and mass activity. This approach is mostly one way, with little interactivity. The consumer database is basic, with limited information, which therefore limits targeting. Marketing spend is used inefficiently without measurable accountability. The marketing plan, if there is one, is primarily product-driven and is unconnected, with no long-term vision or strategy and is driven forward in isolation by a fragmented marketing department. Current activities include product launches, sales promotions, discount push strategies, mass awareness campaigns.

❏ RelModel Level 2 introduces the first steps of consumer interaction and segmentation. Characteristics of this stage are segmenting and targeting consumers by value, style and tone. All consumer information from marketing programmes is held in one central database to enable interactive communication with the consumer. Promotions and mailings can be co-ordinated and responses entered into single consumer database. Strategic marketing plans may be in place but not fully implemented. Companies at this stage are often in the process of absorbing new acquisitions or focusing on new types of consumer.

❑ RelModel Level 3 places the emphasis on personalised service and consumer behavioural aspects. The approach is consumer-driven. Loyalty motivators are known and strategy developed. All previous sales, transactions and contact history are held in the consumer database. From this database, the history is used to give advice and offer suitable sales options. Lifestyle and behaviour information is also stored in the database.

❑ RelModel Level 4 concentrates on advocates (consumers who have become your ambassadors – 'I can thoroughly recommend that brand') and relationship vehicle aspects. This level has loyalty vehicles in place. Benefits are matched to consumer value, motivation and interests. Buying needs and purchasing cycles are increasingly understood. Communication with consumers becomes more individual, frequent and regular.

❑ RelModel Level 5 uses fully integrated, cross selling and maximises consumer relationships and their lifetime value. At this level, lifetime value and consumer profitability are increasingly understood, acted upon and optimised. Partners are linked into communications, marketing and sales activities to enable cross selling. The extensive database is used to widen product offering and perceived sales servicing. Communication to most valuable consumers is highly personalised and based on their stated preferences.

Powering your company up through the RelModel to the fifth and final level is made considerably easier when you make use of the supporting RelModel techniques (I call them RelTechnics, and describe them in detail in Chapter 5) and when you approach the project in an 'All-to-One' way. We are talking breadth of vision – you have to be able to keep the whole process in view, and especially your final target, Level 5. We are also talking integration, interactivity of execution, and making the best use of the synergy innate with every combination of techniques. But you can do it. Remember that it's all been done before, it's all tried and tested, and in fact is comparatively easy – even fun – to implement. Expect to enjoy it. I think you will if you use the help that's available.

The diagram below graphically represents in summary where that help will be needed. In the paragraphs below, I indicate the form that the help takes.

The essential thing is to make sure that your organisational management and culture are outward-looking and consumer-facing. I cover that aspect in full in Chapter 9.

Next (I say, 'next', but all the activity has to move forward together), the enterprise architecture, the way your enterprise is structured, must be consumer-facing, which almost certainly means that it needs re-engineering. I cover that vital topic in Chapter 10.

RelModel and supporting activities

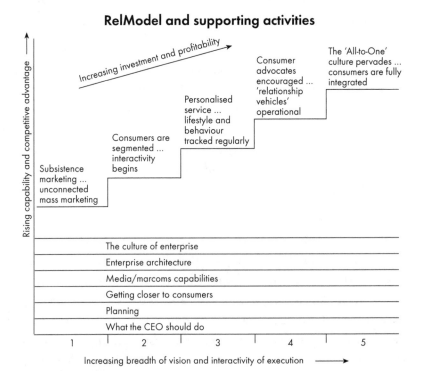

Your marketing communications (Marcoms) must achieve a high level of accuracy and sophistication so as to keep effective focus on the changing and developing moods and modes of your consumer market. I deal with all that in several chapters, most particularly in Chapters 6, 7, 8 and 10. Chapter 6 gives clear-cut advice on how to get the most from the Internet. Chapter 7 surveys every one of the media available to you for consumer communication. Chapter 8 considers the importance of image and brand. Chapter 10, with its integrated marketing model (IMM), shows the key role Marcoms play in all your marketing projects. So does the pull-out 'All-to-One' Journey Pack at the back of the book. I have also included a special section ('A vision of what might be') that elaborates on the difference between a carefully reasoned but uninspired appeal to the target consumer (which rarely works) to the same appeal touched with inspiration. Without inspiration, there's just no point in sending out marketing communications.

Finally, you must see that your company, everyone in it, is constantly working to get closer to the consumer. I deal with that life-or-death subject in Chapter 5 and suggest a range of proven techniques, which I call 'RelTechnics', that will help your company get close enough to the consumer and so consummate that lifelong ambition with your consumers which is the source of lifetime value.

All the preceding paragraphs give the RelModel and its supporting cast in overview only. But before we do go into the all-important detail, let's see the kind of real-life series of events that call for the All-to-One and RelModel treatment:

'You saw the commercial on the box last night.

This morning there was a press ad for the same bit of plastic. It caught your eye – but only just. The chap in the next seat on the tube happened to open his newspaper at the right place and you noticed the headline. And when you looked up you saw something similar on the tube card. Can't escape it. Is someone trying to tell you something?

Then a friend at work said they'd bought the product in question – well, it was one of those ahead-of-the-art mobile phones that link you with the Internet, so they would, wouldn't they? After all, it's pretty high-class plastic. And you talked about it for a bit.

Later in the day, on the way somewhere, you happened to pass a shop window displaying the self-same ahead-of-the-art phone. You thought you might just pop in and have a closer look. The sales person was pleasantly unforceful but forthcoming. The leaflet wasn't too bad either.

The same evening, your husband/partner/boyfriend said wasn't it wonderful what technology could do nowadays and had you seen that new mobile phone which put you on the Internet wherever you wanted wherever you happened to be? Apparently, he said, you could get full details on the Internet, surprise, surprise.

You probably sighed but logged on none the less and sure enough, there it was – all the detail you could possibly want about the new mobile, and more. So between the two of you, you decided to buy one, though perhaps you'd have another look round some of the other outlets before you finally made up your mind.'

So far, the marketing has worked well, although the sale has yet to be clinched. The prospect has been exposed to the advertising in a range of media. She's talked it over with people who've also seen the ads. But is she going to buy? Well, she's human, so you can't be certain.

But you would be more certain that she would buy if the marketing had been shaped on 'All-to-One' principles mediated by the RelModel methodology.

The RelModel allows the individual to be treated as an individual with a name, someone who already has a relationship with the supplier – in this case the WAP phone supplier. If the RelModel methodology had already been in place, the initial impact of the advertising seen by the prospect would have been backed, preceded even, by a personal letter, perhaps by the offer of a free trial, a telephone call at the right time of day, an e-mail, an invite to a launch party. She may even be a regular reader of the company's magazine or a member of its loyalty club. She would remember products and services that she already bought from the same supplier and still enjoys. She would remember the excellent way she was treated. So she would know from experience that the company keeps its promises and that its products are as good as the promises. She would already have been the recipient of special promotions and deals on other products. She would have a firm idea of the character and reliability of the company. She would have been the 'one' in an 'All-to-One' relationship.

All been done before

I can't emphasise enough that there is nothing new about 'All-to-One' or even about the RelModel. The words only supply a label to a process that the most gifted marketers have always applied to their companies and to their products/brands. The point is that in the ruthless, now-or-never competitive world of today we have no time for the long incubation periods necessary in the past to produce brands. Birds Custard, one of the UK's best-known dessert brands, was first launched and advertised over 130 years ago, when Queen Victoria was on the British Throne and Ulysses Grant was President of the USA. The pack has hardly changed. Kellogg first saw the light of day at about the same time, as did Coca-Cola ... and many many more!

Today we don't want to wait a lifetime or longer for results. We want, need results within months not years. And incidentally, no one should assume that today's famous brands will stay famous unless they get their fair share of tender loving care which 'All-to-One' provides. Existing household-name brands need the 'All-to-One' treatment to stay on top just as much as new products need it to achieve the desired brand status. But how do we apply the 'All-to-One' principles to a company and to its products? That's the job of the RelModel.

As I said earlier, 'Rel' is short for 'relationship' because the RelModel is a practical, proven means of implementing CRM – which in turn is a practical, proven means of gaining more consumers and maximising the business to be gained from each one of them. I have been applying the RelModel with major clients in the UK and Europe for several years now and with exceptionally good results. Colleagues in the USA have been doing the same. I should also point out that many successful companies have been using the RelModel without calling it by that name – that's because in fact the RelModel is common sense codified. But whichever – believe me, it works!

It works because it creates and maintains the overall relationship between company and consumer. It works at another level too. It creates, strengthens and sustains the consumer's relationships with your brands. The brands become trusted. Eventually they become trusted friends. I deal with the vitally important matter of 'All-to-One' and brands in Chapter 8, 'Image rules ... brand stays king'.

The RelModel is an evolving journey, a learning curve on how an organisation – *your* organisation – can develop the capabilities that will create a lasting relationship with consumers, lasting and profitable because each consumer gets what he or she most needs – the 'All-to-One' standard of care. But it is not an end in itself. It is an enabler – to enable you and your company to achieve the kind of relationship with consumers that gives them and you lifelong value and, as a result, provides the growth and profit levels that you need.

It also acts as a constant reminder of the goals you have set, a constant encouragement to keep on doing the right thing.

Each of the five levels in the RelModel is a learning experience for your whole enterprise. I have presented the levels in a way that makes it easy for you to decide precisely where you and your company are now. You'll then know what you have to do next! 'Do next' is the hottest advice I can give here. The RelModel works if each of the levels is tackled in the right order. It is cumulative. And don't rush things. Make sure that everyone and everything keeps up to speed. Don't leave anyone or anything behind. If only one part of the organisation is out of sync, the whole project is at risk.

Not every detail on every level applies to every company. As you go through, it will be obvious which apply to you and your company, and which don't. For instance, a supermarket chain will focus on the demographics and psychographics of consumer segments. Likewise a car manufacturer. However, a car dealership will want to sharpen the focus very much on to each individual consumer by name, by very detailed demographics and by even more detailed psychographics.

The system is dynamic – and you have to be dynamic with it. Why? Because as standards increase, so do consumer expectations, and so do the standards of competitors. Yesterday's targets are not enough for today. In practice, this means that you have to meet the requirements of each of the levels with ever-increasing efficiency (I said it was a learning curve). There has to be a disciplined approach to reviewing your achievements at each level – you may have to step back to make sure that the standards achieved at previous levels are acceptable in the light of changes in consumer perceptions and competitor activities (provoked by your activities).

Third-level itch

All this can be even more difficult than it sounds. In my experience of operating the RelModel and watching other people operating it, there is a kind of 'third-level itch'. Companies get halfway through and then get bored ('What's new?'). Some people aren't convinced by the consumer feedback. Someone else needs to make budget cuts. Key people move on. Old habits come back. It's hard to overstate the point: the RelModel can only deliver the goods if it is undertaken with discipline and with the direct involvement of the CEO – whose role is to see that the discipline stays firm. He should also see that it stays flexible. The marketing context is never still, markets change, and although the basic principles remain the same, their implementation may need to be modified if the target is to be achieved. The RelModel assumes intelligence in its practitioners! But let none of this affect the basic point: the RelModel must be seen as a long-term strategy.

But the rewards make it worthwhile, and the rewards come comparatively quickly. If you say, hand on heart, that your company has fulfilled the requirements of Level 1, it will be a better company, more profitable and more likely to succeed than it was before it began. And so on upwards.

A level too far –
How some supermarkets got lost by taking a short cut

The RelModel can't be cheated. It requires companies to start at Level 1 and continue through Levels 2, 3 and 4 before arriving at Level 5. Companies who try the shortcut lose their way.

Here's what happened recently in the UK's never-ending supermarket war.

Tesco, at the time number 2 in the pecking order and aiming to move up by getting even closer to its consumers, had in fact reached Level 4 – though it probably calls it something else. It developed a range of consumer services including a membership card that offers financial services and a range of incentives. Smaller competitors such as Gateway, launched their own me-too 'points-mean-prizes' consumer schemes. However, they hadn't done their homework, hadn't built the capabilities to enable them to segment and use their consumer data. Nor had they built the same consumer-focused culture into their marketing. Tesco, on the other hand, has over 30 different magazines appealing to different consumer groups. They are regularly mailed to relevant consumers. Tesco moved up to number 1. The others saw the membership card and the rest simply as short-term promotional devices – and therefore encouragements to promiscuity, not as the basis for the start of an on-going relationship. Some other competitors, particularly their biggest, Sainsbury's, have continued to invest in long-term consumer relationships also and the battle between them and Tesco for the hearts, minds and an ever-increasing share of consumers' wallets will continue. The rest who haven't understood the battleground will fall away.

At Level 4, the relationship between you and your consumers becomes on-going, completely interactive ('All-to-One-to-all') and as near permanent as anything can be. Consumers 'lock' into the company. As a result, they get the very best the company has to offer and on every dimension. And by being enabled by 'All-to-One' to provide this optimum service, the company can optimise the profit potential of each consumer over a lifetime's relationship – as well as gaining more profit by cross selling and by targeting high-value prospects and winning more of their business again over the whole lifetime. You've achieved optimum 'share of mind' and 'All-to-One' becomes 'All-to-One-to-all' for keeps.

Case study

Merrill Lynch and HSBC

Adding bricks to clicks

WHEN MERRILL LYNCH and HSBC came together to set up the world's first business that combines banking and investment services globally and online, they decided to back the clicks with some good down-to-earth bricks. Says Dave Komansky, Chairman and CEO of the new joint venture: 'The investor we're seeking to reach will have access with one click to sophisticated online financial planning and asset allocation tools.... We'll augment our clicks with bricks, that is physical offices in selected locations – and we'll back up our service with around-the-clock call centers.'

Why have bricks at all? Roberta Arena, Group General Manager for Global E-Business at HSBC answers: 'There's a lot of evidence that dedicated storefronts widen the comfort zone for consumers.' Merrill Lynch Chief Marketing Officer, James Gorman, adds: 'The combination of the pre-eminent online platform, telephone access ... and appropriate storefront access, kiosks, High Street access and the like, we think will be a winning proposition.'

The 50:50 partners are together providing US$1 billion in start-up capital over five years, by when the company should be profitable. They are targeting an initial 10 million consumers (all with investable assets of between US$100,000 and US$500,000) rising to 50 million. The new company wants to maximise its chances of success. As the extracts from the launch press conference indicate, the new company is going to operate on principles that are wholly 'All-to-One'.

Three

The RelModel in full

'To improve is to change, to be perfect is to change often.'

Winston Churchill

W E'VE HAD THE chairperson's summary. This chapter is for the workers! Here we take a detailed look at each level of the RelModel and what it means in terms of everyday business life. This can be categorised as follows: 'The culture of the enterprise'; 'Enterprise architecture'; 'Media/Marcoms'; 'Getting closer to the consumer'; 'Planning' and 'What the CEO should do'. I agree the categories are somewhat arbitrary – in real life the problems spread themselves out more – but they help to make things clearer. Detailed information on 'All-to-One' enterprise culture can be found in Chapter 9, 'Enterprise architecture' in Chapter 10, 'Media/Marcoms' in Chapter 7, and 'Getting closer to the consumer' in Chapter 5. I will use these categorisations to summarise each level.

RelModel Level 1

Dominant characteristics: subsistence marketing; unconnected mass marketing.

Key competitive advantages: You have deeper knowledge of product, a longer experience of the markets than your competitors may have, but the consumers aren't so sure.

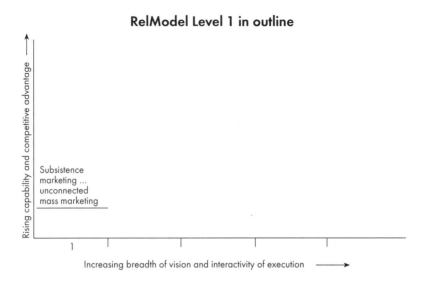

RelModel Level 1 in outline

The guiding principles of companies operating at this level are (a) people are all basically the same; so (b) obviously, you treat them all the same; and (c) people prefer to be told what to buy; so (d) you tell them. The company is boss and the chairperson knows best. After all, the company has unique specialist know-how of its product category and years of experience in providing the products to the market. Is it surprising that the company knows best? Not surprisingly, the big boys (under the chairperson) are all in the financial department. The technology specialists, every kind of technology specialist, product research and manufacturing as well as IT, are the heroes. 'Just look what the research guys have come up with – there's got to be a market for that.' It's the 'we make it, you buy it' at its most pervasive. The company's share of the prospect's mind and its positioning in the prospect's mind are questionable. Its competitive position is weak and it's wide open to attack from more enlightened competitors.

The culture of the enterprise

❏ Everything is driven by the company and/or by the technology, and/or by the product, and/or by the chairperson. The company speaks, the technology shouts, the product demands, the chairperson commands. The consumer can listen, or watch, or read, or buy, or obey, or not, but the communication continues regardless. The consumer has no input except to stay awake when spoken to and produce money on demand. (I exaggerate, but not much.)

❏ The extended enterprise (suppliers, distributors, dealers, agents and other intermediaries) does its own thing with unhappy results – consumers don't distinguish between the company and its extensions.

❏ Very limited authority for most employees.

❏ Lack of clarity about the purpose of the business.

❏ Lack of trust in the management.

❏ Probably a history of downsizing, which says: 'you're just a peg in a hole and we could get rid of you tomorrow'.

❏ Little loyalty. Consumers buy on price and are difficult to retain. Commoditisation is just around the corner.

❏ Difficult to get quick responses or any service which is outside the rulebook. Most commonly heard phrases from an employee are 'It's company policy' and 'I'll have to ask my manager' … from a consumer: 'I bought from them because it was cheap/convenient'.

❏ The company has the capacity to achieve growth but finds it difficult to achieve it because it has only limited vision and limited skill. In addition, in an increasingly fragmented market, the ability and skills required to understand the needs of every niche segment do not exist within the organisation – which makes it difficult to achieve the desired growth. Worse, those competitors who are alert to niche marketing can attack your own consumer base. (It took Land Rover years to realise that its supremacy in the 4×4 off-road, cross-country truck of all trades was being challenged by Japanese and later US niche marketers. They saw a market for this kind of vehicle among city dwellers whose only off-road driving was up the drive to their garage at home.)

❏ The heart of the problem at this level is cultural, and you can't put all the blame on the chairperson. The organisation as a whole is inward looking. Office politics, more flatteringly described as organisational politics, are everywhere, stifling originality, encouraging safety-first, low-risk, yes-sir attitudes. Heads are kept firmly beneath parapets. Nervousness, accompanied by fear, stalks the corridors – we've all experienced that. The safe position to take is: do what was done before and no one can blame you for what happens. If they do, you have an alibi, 'it didn't happen last time'.

Enterprise architecture

❏ All your company's databases are fragmented, contain only basic demographic information and are silo'd up safe from the prying eyes of those who might make good use of them. (Chapter 9 has relevant points to make about the 'silo' phenomenon.)

❏ The consumer data you use, when you use them, are comparatively basic and are poor-quality lists of names and addresses.

❏ Operational databases are dispersed throughout the company, perpetual silos – so consumers are presented with a range of different company faces, and have to give their details again and again.

❏ Oops! Yes and when mistakes in data are seen, there is no way of correcting – as a result, data errors repeat and proliferate.

❏ Enterprise architecture fragmentation is the name of the game.

Media/Marcoms

❏ There is limited strategic input and the long-term implications are not considered. And Marcoms (marketing communications) are always uncoordinated and spurt out from all openings in the company. Your public affairs department tends to do its own thing – in fact you sometimes wonder which company it's working for. Sales have their own messages to deliver – after all, they have targets to meet, so naturally they know best how to make advertising and promotions work to achieve those targets! Retail and distribution have similar ideas. The word 'fragmented' comes to mind … bl**dy disorganised is more the truth – wasteful of resources, dispiriting to the people who work in the company, infuriating to the consumer and to the service people who have to pick up the pieces as best they may. Examples are everywhere in all industries, with the automobile industry providing its fair share – admittedly it has the problem of dealerships often being independently owned and dealerships are still the ultimate consumer-facing contacts. However, the end-results can be chaotic, with dealer publicity quite liable to clash with manufacturer publicity, usually in style and professionalism, but in message too.

❑ Media schedules are shaped on a repetition of past schedules with a cursory glance at analysis such as a basic cost-per-thousand. The content, mood and tone of the media are ignored or dismissed as irrelevant intangibles. The lifestyle characteristics of individual consumers are not known.

❑ The company's media thinking and its attitudes to the measurement of media effectiveness are all entrenched in the past. Its skill sets are those that have been developed and honed through past experience, often successful. The company's organisational capabilities help to perpetuate these traditions. No one can see a light at the end of the tunnel. Not many people realise that they are in a tunnel, one that leads one way to nowhere.

❑ The messages, printed (e.g. press advertisements) or electronic (e.g. TV advertisements), are standardised, product-oriented ('We've made this for you'). If the messages *are* pre-tested, the criteria are 'impact' and 'brand/name recognition'. 'Empathy' and 'persuasiveness' don't come into it.

❏ Brochures and other literature are produced by an agency whose mindset was fixed several decades ago, although a computer 'helps' now. Again, everything is done from the point of view of the product and the company.

❏ Any brand and brand positioning are the results of historical achievements and are being expended rather than invested in.

❏ Information provided to the consumer in any medium is kept to a minimum – on a kind of 'need to know' basis. In any event, the company attitude is that 'people soon get bored reading about products, so why bother?'

❏ The company gets an outside direct mail agency to mail brochures to consumers or prospects at addresses supplied from outside the company. Recipients are divided into broad categories based on criteria, mainly demographic, devised by the outside supplier who, being born and bred in the direct mail industry, finds it easier to perpetuate its endemic mistakes. This is a good step in the right direction, but little or no advantage is taken of the company's own knowledge of the market and the consumers in it. The lists, although with some de-duplication, are not particularly up to date, liable to mistakes and produce too many 'gone-aways'. However, you won't know that. You can't expect a direct mail agency to report back its failure.

❏ On the website (where inter-activity should be the norm), only fixed information is given, often taken straight from the Annual Report (which shows that the PR department runs the site – PR departments are fond of Annual Reports). It is the electronic brochure at its most. It tends not be updated. It often crashes.

❏ There is a strong emphasis on above-the-line advertising, press and TV, with possibly coupon response facilities in the press ads.

❏ Promotions are on a one-off, ad-hoc basis. They are little more than knee-jerk reactions to particular issues recognised at board level and/or to unexpected crises in the marketplace – perhaps competitors' activity which no one had been monitoring, or a change in direction by consumers.

❏ Little response analysis is carried out to check the cost-effectiveness of advertising and marketing activity – and, if any, it usually carried out by the outside agencies responsible for the activity and who tend only to report good news.

Getting closer to consumers

❏ Understanding is far from widespread within the company and it is based on historical perspectives, that is on samples of the past rather than on the actual buying behaviour of your real consumers.

❏ Information on consumers is held in a variety of places, some of them unexpected, and often in paper format. Those who hold the information guard it jealously, they may be genuinely fearful of its misuse. More likely, they look upon it as part of their patch. Others keep off – although the others are not even aware of its existence.

❏ There is no real segmentation or understanding of consumer behaviour, buying processes or consumer emotions and trends.

Planning

❏ Certainly there is forward planning, usually on the basis of last-year-plus-a-percentage, after all tomorrow will soon be here. But there is no vision beyond tomorrow, no strategic marketing plan, nothing long term or lifelong. Tomorrowland really will turn up tomorrow and not the day after!

❑ Perhaps there really is an overall marketing plan, limited though it may be. Most, but not all, marketing activity is coordinated which allows for some information gathering. Promotions tend to slip through the net.

What the CEO should do

❑ Lead in a way that clearly communicates the purpose of the organisation.

❑ Reward good service providers.

❑ Shout about the importance of consumers.

❑ Get rid of attitudes and processes that block service.

❑ Have fewer rules.

❑ Devolve authority to make decisions outside the rules.

❑ Establish effective systems and processes to understand consumer segments.

Is this your company? Is this you? You probably recognise some of the behaviour but no organisation fits exactly into a level cleanly – even the best of companies have odd spots of trouble and even the worst can point to some virtues. The trick is to recognise where the behaviour and the capabilities of your company most relate to those described above. If you decide that, by and large, Level 1 is where you're at, then it's time to move up to Level 2.

RelModel Level 2

Dominant characteristic: consumers are segmented and interactivity begins.

Key competitive advantages: you have a more precise understanding of consumer lifestyles and hence you're on your way to a larger share of consumers' minds than your competitors have.

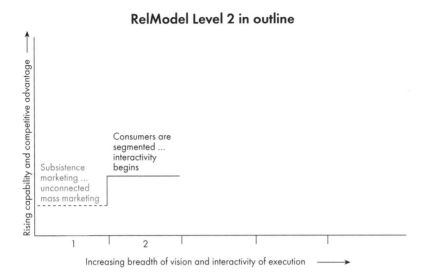

RelModel Level 2 in outline

To achieve this level the prerequisite is that you have learnt from your marketing activity in Level 1. You have put the metrics in your campaigns and the measurement provides learning opportunities for improving your targeting and campaigns in the future. You're getting closer to your consumers, analysing your data, segmenting into consumer groups and starting to talk and to get interactive.

At this level, you have the capacity to measure consumers' lifestyles sufficiently well to segment them into groups with tastes, preferences, habits and attitudes that are special to them – though their behaviour patterns are not yet measured. The company appreciates that it has to treat consumer groups in a way that complements their lifestyle. The company's competitive standing is now more firmly based. It holds a larger share of the prospect's mind, is less open to attack and more capable of counter-attack.

What all this means in terms of everyday business life can be categorised as follows:

The culture of the enterprise

❏ Cross-functional communication and coordination within the company is greatly improved with all functions focusing on the objectives and feeling involved in the whole marketing scene.

❏ Some departments are more important than others.

❏ Among some sections of the company there is an understanding of consumer profiles and of typical consumer decision/buying processes.

❏ Still inward-looking: consumers seen as out there lurking in segmented groups, but things are changing.

❏ All functions within the company participate or begin to participate (as appropriate) in creating and implementing the strategic marketing plan between servicing and marketing functions.

Enterprise architecture

❏ Employees are still easily replaced.

❏ The enterprise architecture detailed in Chapter 10 is coming into shape.

❏ All consumer information from whatever source is now held on one central database – accessible, incidentally, to all departments.

❏ The information is used to segment consumers into different groups with similar lifestyles and other marketing characteristics (a good start).

❏ The previous buying behaviour of consumers is tracked, and the information stored.

❏ Each consumer identified with a unique consumer ID.

❏ Telephone sales support teams are put in place to follow up enquiries and maintain the consumer database quality.

Media/Marcoms

❏ Promotions and mailings are coordinated and responses entered into a single consumer database.

❏ Separate marketing activities are carried out for different segments. For instance, new prospects are exposed to their own specially tailored promotional offers, which are different from those offered to current consumers.

❏ Separate mailings are created and dispatched to different segments of the target market.

❏ Up-to-date lists of consumers are maintained, with special attention paid to the accuracy of titles and addresses and carefully identified profile details.

❏ This means that personalised 'salutations' can be used in all consumer communications and contacts with the consumer, including those contacts made by the telephone at the company's offices or at the call centre. The company now realises that there is no quicker way of infuriating someone than to allow a communication cock-up (that's the technical phrase) at the call centre or at the office or at the retail outlet. 'Hello Mrs Smith' gets no prizes from Miss Jones or even Ms Jones. In written communications, great care is taken to ensure the correct spelling of people's names (and addresses).

❏ Quality is recognised and things are being done about it.

❏ All consumer communications, including advertising, now projects the same brand/company image. So do all person-to-person communications at the office, call centre or selling outlet. The vital importance of a whole-company culture is accepted and acted on.

Getting closer to consumers

❏ The company understands the *context* in which the communication is sent out. In other words, the timing and content of the communication reflects known facts about the recipient – birthdays or anniversaries, new business/new job, just married, new house, car for business versus car for family use, the events in people's lives that could make them more or less responsive to your message, its tone and its timing.

❑ Consumers are important and consumer information comes first.

❑ The company seems to want to understand more about you (the consumer) so you'll receive some questionnaires. You'll then get information about products 'for people like you'. Consumers who don't fit into its range of segments or product 'boxes' are difficult to service.

❑ 'I bought it from them and I'm pretty sure it's alright'.

Planning

❑ A strategic marketing plan is now in place but not fully implemented.

What the CEO should do

❑ Keep shouting that the consumer is No. 1.

❑ Start shouting that employees are important too.

❑ Develop human resources (HR) policies and training which treats employees as individuals and adults, e.g. introduce flexible reward systems.

❑ Encourage risk and reward new ideas.

❑ Set challenges for informal teams.

❑ Encourage coaching and learning by doing.

Does your company share some or most of the characteristics set out above? If so, it's high time you moved on to Level 3. You have this rather obvious consolation. You wouldn't be able to move up to Level 3 if you weren't already at Level 2. And Level 3 is only two from the top!

RelModel Level 3

Dominant characteristic: personalised service. Lifestyle and behaviour are now tracked regularly.

Key competitive advantage: you understand consumers' buying habits better than your competitors do.

RelModel Level 3 in outline

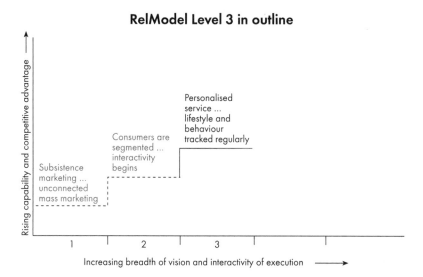

Level 3 is a good level to be at – provided you don't stay there too long! Companies here are in much better shape to strengthen their competitive position. They become more creative in every way and the creativity is better focused. They appreciate that it is vital to track consumer behaviour on a regular basis, to get to understand consumer moods and buying modes (who buys, where, when, how), to match products and promotion to specific consumer lifestyles, and altogether treat consumers as 'rounded' personalities with a life outside the company's own products! They continue to increase their share of the consumers' minds in the right way. Consequently, they are creating an organisational structure and a complex of attitudes that will be the best guarantee for long-term growth. Capabilities in the organisation are growing: skills in managing people, skills in using the different media, skills in managing data and systems.

What all this means in terms of everyday business life can be
categorised as follows.

The culture of the enterprise

❏ The company and its activities are now consumer-driven. This is
possible because the company takes increasing care to retain and
categorise all relevant demographic and psychographic
information about each consumer.

❏ Increasing focus on project teams or problem-solving groups.

❏ All your people have clear pictures of your consumers and are
proud to be part of the team, morale is high and upward – but you
need to keep on it.

❏ Innovation is good.

❏ Taking some measured risks is acceptable.

❏ Flexibility is valued in responses and in individuals ('We could
try it').

❏ As an employee, you will feel a sense that the company actually
cares if you as an individual are not happy. You'll give them
feedback and feel sure it will be acted upon.

Enterprise architecture

❏ The integrated marketing model described in Chapter 10 is in
place and fully working giving continual improvement to the
efficiency of marketing operations and communications to the
company.

❏ The company systematically tracks all aspects of the consumer's
lifestyle, including buying patterns. There is a high level of
consumer personalisation with likes, dislikes, foibles, interests,
hobbies, potential for new ideas all charted.

❏ All lifestyle information together with associated behavioural information is held on the database.

❏ Research is carried out into the decision-to-buy process in each segment and the results of the research made available to all in the company who need it, as well as all in the company who express interest.

❏ Everyone in the company is enabled to treat consumers as people not as numbers on a chart. (There is an important staff relationship point here. Those working inside an organisation adapt their view of the organisation from the way it treats its consumers. I'll slightly overstate the case to make the point: if an organisation treats it consumers with contempt, members of staff will soon treat the company with contempt too.)

❏ Details of all previous transactions by the consumer are held on the database. So are details of the whole history of the consumer's relationships at all levels with the company from the very first contact -- including requests for help or information, complaints about the product or the service, compliments, however slight and, hopefully, however all-embracing. This information is used to devise new selling approaches to different consumer segments.

❏ Purchases by your consumers of competitive products are difficult to track with anything like complete accuracy, but the company is now making an effort to do so. This information, particularly if accompanied by the reasons for the competitive purchase, is an invaluable addition to the consumer profile.

❏ The database-held history of transactions by each consumer is used to frame the precise purchase options offered to that consumer. Although they know by now that the whole process depends on computers and not the memory of individuals within the company, consumers are still pleased to be made offers that are logical and that seem a thoughtful follow-up to previous purchasing decisions that they have made. (To put it in everyday, pre-marketing-speak language: canny Mr Peacock in the village shop, knows that Mrs Vicar likes a bit of exotic cheese from time to time and has occasionally bought some from him in the past. He suggests that she might like to try some of this Port Salut — 'it's just come in and it's in prime condition'. Bet she buys it.)

❏ Inventory management is now improved because of the better match between demand and volume production.

❏ All sales leads are held on the database and every contact with consumers continues to be logged.

❏ 'All-to-One' enterprise architecture puts relevant information at the point of sale, so that where possible personalised service can be delivered.

❏ The consumer database is available to all sales staff (and indeed to everyone else in the company who wants it) and is routinely used by everyone before making any contact with consumers or prospects.

Media/Marcoms

❏ Mailings of all kinds are tightly targeted to meet the requirements of each consumer segment and to coordinate with life stages and key events.

❏ Promotions are specific to known target groups within segments and they are invitation-based, that is prospects are asked beforehand if they would like to take part.

❏ Sales material is designed and held in such a way that it can be produced on demand in a customised form suitable for one particular consumer.

❏ Website tools are added to help buying decisions. For instance, if your product is a car, a caravan, a boat or other piece of capital equipment, the consumer is empowered to buy accessories on-screen. If your product is such that a consumer may need special finance, this too can be made available on-screen.

❏ The website is now interactive and designed to take consumer preferences and consumer profile into account. Consumers find the site easier to navigate. Maybe they are greeted by name each time they visit the site.

❏ Plenty of personalised tools and services.

❏ Your capabilities are well developed to use a wide variety of media in a controlled and professional manner, with metrics and improvement cycles built in. The integrated marketing model is in place and you are increasing your Marcoms efficiency with every move.

❏ You are no longer relying on a number of disparate agencies each taking the lead in their own specialisation and with their own agenda – you are now the conductor and the different sections all follow your beat.

❏ Integration of all your media and campaigns is now kicking in substantial bottom-line measurable benefits.

❏ Your 'All-to-One' Journey Maps become ever more sophisticated.

Getting closer to consumers

❏ Every part of the organisation is focusing on the consumer.

❏ The factors that motivate and maintain consumer loyalty are now much better known and understood. Strategies are evolved to take more advantage of this knowledge/understanding.

❏ The company now understands and is able to act on the key events and life stages of each consumer.

❏ Pro-active mailings timed to link with the buying cycles of different consumer segments and with different times of the year – Christmas, vacations, school holidays, onset of winter and the like.

❏ The total interaction between consumer and company – purchasing, servicing, enquiries, complaints, congratulations, response to direct mail, exposure to media advertising and point of sale, attendance at events (such as a wine tasting) – is tracked, recorded and accessible throughout the company.

❏ Better knowledge and understanding of the changing motivations of individual consumers allow promotions to be mounted quickly in response to competitor aggression and/or to ensure that short- or long-term business needs and targets are met.

❏ The company now knows enough about individual consumers to predict each consumer's value to the company over a five-year period, or longer. This information is held in the database. The acquisition of this knowledge and its use represent a major boost for the company's prospects. They enable strategic objectives to be defined with much more precision and can dramatically strengthen the morale of the whole company. Suddenly, the road ahead seems well mapped and the destination completely clear.

❏ The loyalty of each consumer is carefully tracked.

Planning

❏ Long-term nature of decision/buying cycle is recognised and communications geared to each stage (after sales, maintenance, information gathering to make next purchase).

❏ Different targets are set for each stage of the buying process.

❏ New business activity is based on a very good understanding of current consumer profile.

❏ Loyalty promotional schemes for different groups are devised and in place. They are not only relevant to the groups but support the overall strategic direction.

❏ Servicing recognised as an important part of the selling process.

❏ Marketing activity moving to one-to-one basis for the most highly valued consumers.

❏ There is a much better media mix – to match the greater understanding of how each group of consumers reacts to different media and media combinations. For example there tends to be less above-the-line activity but it is better targeted, with closer media matches linked to target mood and mode (i.e. where they are, what they are doing) when exposed to the messages.

What the CEO should do

❏ Remember that consumers prefer to be treated like people.

❏ Invite the 'voice of the consumer' into your organisation.

❏ Put 'consumer' as the first item on all meeting agendas.

❏ Lead in a way that practises what you preach.

❏ Keep shouting that both the consumer and the employee are No. 1.

❏ Provide more strategic information for your employees and get them involved in planning the future.

❏ Reduce the number of managers.

❏ Have more team managers and project groups.

❏ Erase demarcation lines.

❏ Encourage a cross-functional approach to problems and opportunities.

If you can relate all or most of the above to your company, congratulations – you're on your way. You're working for a good company. Your organisation starts to become attack-proof. You can see the attacks coming because you are accurately tracking those changes in consumer buying habits that trigger the attacks. You also have the ability to react quickly, with more accuracy and with greater assuredness of the results of your initiatives. You can have a lot of confidence in your people, your processes and your systems. Best of all, the top is in sight. You have only to fulfil the conditions required of Level 4 companies. Use what you've learnt from Level 3 to catapult your company to a new level of competitive advantage.

RelModel Level 4

Dominant characteristics: consumer advocates encouraged; 'relationship vehicles' operational; internal consumer champions appointed; two-way communication with consumers the norm.

Key competitive advantages: you know better than your competitors do about how to respond to consumer preferences for the types of relationships they want; you are able to wrap a protecting relationship and loyalty field around your consumers; your competitors have to battle with your advocate consumers as well as your self.

RelModel Level 4 in outline

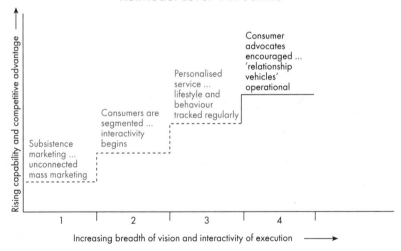

The learning curve steepens! The company now accepts that consumers know best. What all this means in terms of everyday business life can be categorised as follows.

The culture of the enterprise

❏ Less sense of 'us and them'.

❏ Replaced by almost a pride in 'our consumers'.

❏ The culture is self-perpetuating and dominated by constant change and refocus to consumer needs.

❏ Contact can start with the consumer or the company, and the company knows which is which.

❏ Responses to competitive moves are instant – from the bottom up.

❏ Problem solving is seen as part of the job.

❏ Roles are much less clearly defined internally.

❏ Watch out for arrogance with non-'insiders'.

❏ As a consumer, you will, occasionally, feel as if being a consumer of this organisation makes you more special in some way. You will want to recommend it all the time and will almost feel affronted if others criticise it.

❏ And you will give it the benefit of the doubt when it doesn't perform for a while.

❏ But you will feel betrayed if this continues.

❏ The company's culture is now fully oriented to the consumer and not to the product or any other internal focus.

❏ Everyone in every department (including accounts and any 'third-party' suppliers) is trained, encouraged and motivated to 'project' consistently the company's personality (otherwise known as 'image') in every contact with consumers, prospects and the outside world generally. Everyone is now a brand ambassador.

❏ The company is now fully committed to becoming a consumer-led organisation and to creating a culture that implements that commitment. The company's infrastructure is shaped to the same end. Cross-functional teams involving senior management, finance, research, production, IT, sales, marketing, advertising and public affairs work together to serve particular consumer segments. Induction courses and training and refresher programmes all centre on the consumer.

❏ The flirtation and courtship stages are in the past, you are now 'married'. You must not let your partner down, otherwise there will be separation leading to divorce with the final settlement not in your favour! But if you work at it – and we shouldn't take the analogy too far! – you can look forward to a productive and mutually profitable relationship for life.

Enterprise architecture

❏ All information about each consumer is accessible throughout the company and across all functions.

❏ As a result, marketing and branding is integrated across the company with consequent increase in effectiveness and reduction in costs.

❏ The enterprise now has the ability developed at Levels 2 and 3 to achieve the quality standards required to make these schemes work.

❏ All communication systems are fully integrated and every consumer contact is recorded.

Media/Marcoms

❏ 'Loyalty' schemes are launched with full support teams in place. All those involved are fully trained and motivated to achieve all the scheme's objectives.

❏ Two-way consumer communication is encouraged, particularly with the most valued, lifetime consumers.

❏ Consumers are contacted with sales and other material through the communication channels they prefer.

Getting closer to consumers

❏ Interactivity via the website and the call centre lets consumers give their input on the benefits, whether they concern new products, new financial deals, new servicing arrangements or whatever. All the benefits can be fine-tuned to meet individual consumer preferences.

❏ This interactivity throws further light on buying needs and purchasing cycles.

❏ Each consumer's family and circle of friends can now be targeted, although, of course, always with permission, relevance, discretion and courtesy.

❏ You now know enough about your consumers to design and implement the most relevant relationship vehicle to various groups within your consumer base. You know how they want to shop to fit their lifestyle. You know what type of interaction with your organisation or brand suits them, suits their lifestyle. You can now decide what vehicle is best suited to the type of relationship your consumers would prefer. This vehicle can be a mix of communication, distribution and transactional elements – it will have a mix of main media and secondary support media – such as a club card, a credit card, a Christmas club, a catalogue, a shop, a sales person, a loose network of agents, a television programme, an Internet vehicle, whatever. You are now close enough to the consumer to determine which will work best.

❏ Segmentation of consumers is now made on the basis of current profitability, influence and lifelong value.

❏ Consumers feel increasingly confident about the company, approve of its endeavours to establish two-way contact and as a result, feel known, valued and involved.

❏ The consumer relationship is further strengthened through a range of specially tailored benefits, including promotions, offers and insider information.

❏ Relationship vehicles, loyalty clubs and subscription services are now up and running, with consumers happy to be involved.

❏ Consumers feel increasingly confident about the company, approve of its endeavours to establish two-way contact and as a result, feel known, valued and involved.

❏ The consumer relationship is further strengthened through a range of specially tailored benefits, including promotions and offers.

❏ The benefits are shaped in line with the estimated lifetime value of each consumer. They also reflect particular consumers' motivations and interests.

❏ Services to consumers are personalised, tailored to needs and driven by individual consumers.

❏ You now have 'consumer champions', people in the company whose job it is to concentrate on one particular consumer segment and ensure that their interests are fully met in all that the company does. For instance, if 'mothers with children under the age of 2' is one of your consumer segments, then their champion would see to it that appropriate funds were devoted to the development of products suitable for that consumer segment – that's obvious. Perhaps a less obvious task of the 'young mothers' champion would be to ensure that other products made by the company did not present hazards or temptations to babies at the crawling-everywhere stage or that company advertising for other products did not project a lifestyle which young mothers might find objectionable.

❏ The minimum number of contacts for each consumer/prospect grouping is established, together with the particular type of communication for each individual.

❏ The consumer's family is included in the marketing activity wherever appropriate (it usually is).

Planning

❏ Strategic marketing plan covers each key market segment and consumer grouping, with market share and growth targets for each segment and grouping.

❏ All promotional and communication activity is concentrated on maximising the 'all-life' of each consumer.

❏ Where after-sales service is appropriate, it becomes an important element of the total product offered. This lays the foundation for lifetime value, a state of affairs reached at Level 5.

❏ Long-term consumer relationships based on the added value resulting from product and service quality are now the aim and increasingly the norm.

What the CEO should do

❏ Insist on 'total service and total commitment – *all* of the time'.

❏ Move away from job titles and dramatically reduce role clarity.

❏ Have far fewer executives.

❏ Get more people spending time with consumers and out of the office, including you!

❏ Share more information than you would normally want to.

❏ Ask more questions to generate possibilities from your staff.

❏ Reward relationship maintenance.

❏ Stop calling them consumers and start thinking of them as partners.

❏ Work in more joint ventures and partnerships to provide consumer solutions.

If you, representing your company, can nod through all the above points, you're ready for the final level. You're about to arrive! But please don't think that when you've arrived you can relax! The five levels do indeed make a learning curve that can bring you to a full appreciation of what is needed to succeed in our hyper-competitive new Internet-plus economy. But beware, that economy intends to stay 'new', which means that it will continue to change. I believe that the learning methodology contained in the five stages will enable you and your company to stay ahead of whatever the ever-new Internet-plus economy can throw at you.

Relmodel Level 5

Dominant characteristic: the 'All-to-One' culture pervades. Consumers are fully integrated.

Key competitive advantage: you have a 'lifetime value' relationship with each of your consumers; they protect the company, they direct the way, they are ahead of the competition, they will often act as advocates for the company and its products. You can now maximise the 'share of wallet' and lifetime value through cross-selling based on a strong and long-term relationship.

RelModel Level 5 in outline

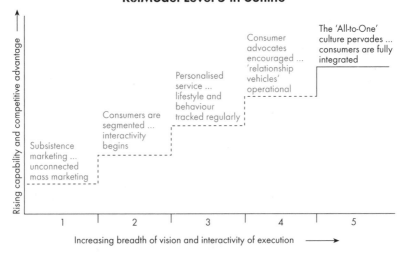

Level 5 is a good place to be. You've not only achieved full 'All-to-One' status, but also you understand how you achieved it, and so have a good idea how to *keep* it. (But don't even think of relaxing.) At Level 5 consumers have become friends for life – you could say married for life. OK, to talk about 'marriage' with a company and its products is way over the top, but useful as a guide to behaviour. The notion of 'friendship' is also a good guide and quite close to reality too. Just think for a moment of the best car you've ever owned, or the sharpest marmalade you've ever tasted, or the happiest holiday you and your family have ever taken. Of course, you can't be friends with a car or a marmalade or a holiday destination or the providers of those commodities in quite the same way as with another human being. But you can feel pleasure at the thought of them, nostalgia when you see or read about them, delight when someone offers them to you again, and loyalty when someone poor-mouths them. Such responses are truly the characteristics of human friendship.

But, whatever the words you use to describe it, this is the relationship you enjoy at Level 5. You hold an optimum share of mind with your consumers. But remember, this relationship, this friendship needs be kept continually in good repair. This consumer loyalty and the favourable emotions that accompany it, all boosted by your own marketing skills and experience, are now the driving forces of your company's success. But they will only continue to work for you if they are kept in good repair.

Level 5 is a state of mind. There is a continual renewing of the strength of the consumer/company relationship, a constant determination to burnish the image, strengthen the brand you have developed in the minds of your consumers. They are now your champions. But you have to keep driving forward to develop the next idea, the next improvement to the product or service. The good news is that your consumers are with you, leading the way, telling you what they want, what they have seen elsewhere and think you could do better. The conduits, the consumer champions you put in place in Level 4, are now well embedded into the culture of the organisation. The momentum can be maintained.

Level 5 is truly the 'end-game' competitive strategy. You can now target new consumer segments, enter new industries even, with the confidence that you have competitive weapons that any adversary, new or old, would fear.

What all this means in terms of everyday business life can be categorised as follows.

The culture of the enterprise

❏ The company is now fully committed to being a consumer-led organisation and to creating a culture that implements that commitment. The company's infrastructure is shaped to the same end. Cross-functional teams involving senior management, finance, research, production, IT, sales, marketing, advertising and public affairs work together to serve particular consumer segments and consumer groups. Induction courses and training and refresher programmes all centre on the consumer.

❏ The enterprise's culture and its sense of community within itself and within the extended enterprise have become self-perpetuating. All your people feel part of this community. So do your suppliers, dealers, advisors, agencies and all other partners.

❏ Your consumers determine the direction the company takes (the recent Ford UK slogan 'Everything we do is driven by you' neatly summarises the situation). Consumers lead the way, develop the next product or service in concept at least.

❏ The selling emphasis turns now and more than ever before on the lifelong benefits to be gained from an on-going special relationship between consumer and company. Selling product is no longer an aim in itself. What is important is the special relationship. For instance, the special relationship of a company supplying fuel for central heating is not simply about the equipment, the servicing and the fuel but on the special relationship which puts responsibility for heating the consumer's home in exactly the way and at the price the consumer wants –

and always. A motor manufacturer sells mobility, style, safety, etc., not just a car. Like practically everything else in marketing, this is an old idea, but its application is new and the ability to apply it in the ever-more complex and mega-competitive Internet-plus economy is the challenge. Never before has a company been able to know sufficient about each and every consumer to enter into a sustainable relationship for life. It can now.

❏ The enterprise sees itself as part of an extended organism or ecosystem that includes consumers, suppliers, agents, potential partners and both current and ex-employees.

❏ On-going relationships and taking care of them are seen as vital for both staff and consumers.

❏ Fluid 'why not' approaches to new challenges are everywhere: ever thought of 'instant pilots'? Try and see what happens (don't let them leave the ground until you're satisfied they know how to get back again).

❏ There is no such thing as sales and marketing – it is a part of everyone's lifestyle.

Enterprise architecture

❏ A fully integrated, multi-modal enterprise architecture is in place – it is fully homogenised with consumers and the extended organisation.

❏ All relevant information about each consumer continues to be collected, stored and categorised, and is kept completely updated.

❏ Information about each consumer is 'translated' into a rounded profile and available to all.

All information about each consumer is regularly examined to identify opportunities for reaching new consumer segments and for developing existing and new products to that individual.

Media/Marcoms

❏ All communication with the most highly valued consumers is highly personalised and based on their known preferences and interests.

Getting closer to consumers

❏ Loyalty benefits and special offers of all kinds are offered to consumers across the company's full range of products and services.

❏ But no one forgets that the basic benefits – quality, added value and service – must always be there.

❏ The consumer relies on you to keep him/her supplied with the latest but proven products. The lifelong consumer must never feel left behind. 'New and bold – and out with the old' is blazoned on the banners, always checking first that the consumer does not actually prefer the old!

Planning

❏ Priority is now with the consumer.

❏ With a relationship offering lifelong potential established in one product field, similar relationships in other fields can be explored. Cross selling becomes comparatively easy. The trust built up in the first relationship will make the second aim easier to achieve.

❏ Being a consumer of this organisation is almost one of the things which defines you as a person …

… you feel they know you and that their main interest is to 'help' you achieve your own needs in this area.

… you find it difficult to imagine changing to any other provider.

… when in doubt, you will speak to them because even if you're not sure it's what they do, you know they will find some way to help.

What the CEO should do

❏ Insist on total service and total commitment – always.

❏ Keep checking that the organisation's mouth and feet are doing the same thing.

❏ Remember that you can always slip back.

❏ Continue to test everything, be open to new ideas, question existing ones.

❏ Meet consumers daily.

❏ Be seen to be focusing on consumers' needs and problems.

❏ Be seen to be not complacent.

❏ Keep challenging people for new ideas.

❏ Be seen to be rewarding people.

❏ Do all the things you have learnt at each of the preceding levels.

Case study

The British utility industry

Multi-utility one-stop marketing activity – the greatest lost marketing opportunity

T HE UTILITY MARKET is only now coming to terms with the twenty-first century and with the kind of competition it has never experienced before. Regarded for years as a commodity, hiding under the protection of government rules and regulations, the industry over the last four years has been experiencing rapid change with regard to a new open marketplace.

What does that mean for the consumer?

Well, choice of supplier and choice of flexible tariffs and payment schemes, for one. The work I started six years ago as head of marketing for Scottish Power was all about developing a new range of multi-utility offers and related services and products that could be packaged and sold not only to the existing consumer base but also to new prospects.

To capitalise on this proposition the utility market has, through government intervention, been forced to deregulate so that now both business and domestic consumers can select which supplier they want to buy their utilities from. The fact is that overall the utilities are not good at marketing, CRM or follow-up with the exemption of some of the 'telcos'.

Much effort has been spent in trying to reposition the old electricity boards into fast-moving consumer-focused multi-utility brands capable of delivering multi-utility product offers all from one point of contact.

The fact is that the mindset of these companies is still heavily stuck in the old regional electricity management approach of using the billing function as the only means of consumer contact.

Unfortunately that mindset is still present.

Little contact is made by the new look utility companies to contact their existing consumers and the approach to recruit new

Case study (continued)

consumers is done in the traditional method of using large-scale advertising campaigns as opposed to more targeted communication.

To complicate this even further the overall consumer approach to switching suppliers is much like their relationship with their banks, that is they lock themselves by their own inertia.

Coupled with this fact is the rise of the Internet aggregators who are selling multi-utility packages online and as a result are bringing the product offer back to where it was several years ago as a commodity offer. The value proposition of the one-stop shop, all utilities under one roof, has been traded off against the lowest priced (and therefore the lowest cost operator/supplier).

Where they got it wrong

In general a total lack of understanding of the power of the consumer database, to segment, profile and design value-added services that would generate greater profit opportunities for the supplier.

With the exception of a few, most utility companies do little to prompt active outbound selling initiatives. Little cross selling is done and the opportunity to develop relationship marketing partners as with the airlines has been lost. At worst those who have gone down this route, such as Centrica/AA only seem to be playing at the idea as opposed to offering tangible consumer benefits. Their offers are no more than putting other brands in touch with like-minded consumers as opposed to actively forging together strategic partnerships that would add value to a consumer relationship and in effect tie people into the proposition of remaining loyal to the utility company.

The emergence of the Internet players over the last year in the UK will create in effect a greater move towards product and service 'commoditisation' and will allow their range of products and services to be easily copied by any new entrant coming into the utility market environment.

Brand switching has been made easier by the touch of a button. The inept and inert approach to CRM delivery and execution seems to be in the process of gathering pace as the utility company is becoming more remote from its true end user.

Case study (continued)

The ability to offer a multi-utility offer to an existing consumer base such as Sainsbury's or British Airways may allow the host company to exploit more profitable consumer relationships than the utility company. Why? Well cost to market, coupled with small profit margins and the lack of investment over the last four/five years in integrated consumer database management programmes, has kept the utility industry very much on the back foot with regard to profitable exploitation of its consumer base.

Lessons learned

Little use of outbound telemarketing call centres for cross selling products and services.

No service differentiation as all consumers are treated the same as there is no facing database system in place to manage the process of consumer segmentation in terms of managing the most and least profitable consumers.

Inability to reposition themselves with their consumers to offer more tangible products and services that provide greater brand equity and therefore brand saliency.

Inability to measure CLTV (consumer lifetime value) as the database they use for any consumer communication is based on billing records and consolidation rather than outgoing sales and marketing channel management strategy.

New Internet offers will encourage more shopping around for prices as consumers will trade off service benefits against price. In effect the utilities have 'painted themselves into a corner'.

This case study was compiled by my colleague, Chris Owens.

Virgin

THE VIRGIN GROUP has been particularly adept at leveraging its first success in one area (the music industry) to create success in others. The Group has taken risks to do it. Normally, people are averse to dealing with the same supplier on a continuing basis for product types that differ greatly from each other. Virgin began by selling recorded music, then moved into air transport, rail transport, soft drinks, financial services, contraceptives and radio stations – it's hard to think of a stranger mixture. It seems to work, held together no doubt by the public perception of the Virgin brand as the consumers' champion, which in turn reflects people's perception of Richard Branson – whom consumers respect and rely on to behave in a certain way, someone they can trust to act on their behalf. But the general rule is to keep the product/service areas within speaking distance of each other. A car manufacturer can offer accessories and insurance with complete conviction but should be warned off food.

However, the fact remains that by linking the unlinkable, Richard Branson has created the only new 'world-known' company to come out of the UK for 20 years or more. His success underlines the point that a risk-taking company with energy and charisma can buck the rules and win, and that logical, sensible marketing by the book is no more than the springboard from which genius can take off. No, genius is too strong. But the most successful marketing does depend finally on there being a touch of genius, a flash of brilliance, a piercing insight, or just luck, I go into this fascinating area more thoroughly on page 171 in the section headed 'A vision of what might be'. But not even genius can work unless the organisational and marketing foundations have been properly prepared. Richard Branson isn't just a pretty face. There's hard marketing thinking going on in the brain behind.

B2B needs 'All-to-One'

T HIS BOOK IS about marketing to the individual, seeking to satisfy his or her personal needs and wants. Marketing to the individual must be 'All-to-One' or it will fail. But the principles – and the threats – apply equally in business-to-business (B2B) marketing.

Of course, in B2B the 'All' includes a much greater helping of specification, price, delivery, all of them 'measurable' and the 'One' is a professional specialist company perfectly capable of 'measuring' what is received, compare it with what was ordered and if it isn't, pursue the supplier until the order is properly fulfilled.

This rock-bottom competence enables any company to join with others in open trading communities on the Internet, where buyers and sellers come together to facilitate and accelerate the exchanges of goods and services. As a result, operational costs are reduced and efficiency increased. The entire goods and services supply chain can be automated.

The prizes are worth having because they include strategic competitive advantages as well as a rapid return on investment. For companies, the Internet is essentially an open marketplace where value flows from speed, service and 'connectedness' between every buyer and every seller. The economists have long asserted that perfect markets can't exist. True, but in B2B the Internet comes close. Shell and General Motors are just two of the thousands, perhaps millions of companies who are now saving time and money through Internet trading.

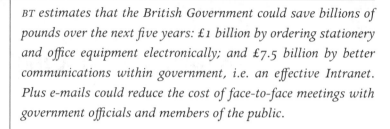

> BT *estimates that the British Government could save billions of* *pounds over the next five years: £1 billion by ordering stationery* *and office equipment electronically; and £7.5 billion by better* *communications within government, i.e. an effective Intranet.* *Plus e-mails could reduce the cost of face-to-face meetings with* *government officials and members of the public.*

IBM's Louis V. Gerstner puts the point well: 'The Net overturns existing business models and obliterates age-old barriers to entry; it will move on to transform market structures and create entirely new kinds of markets. This applies to markets of all kinds – for goods and services, commodities, capital, health-care services, education and skilled labour. These e-marketplaces are attempting to challenge – and potentially dismantle – many of the inherent structural inefficiencies that prevail in any physical market. Simple things: like incomplete information about supply and demand and pricing, or the impossibility of all buyers finding and negotiating with every potential seller.'

Dick Brown, Chief Executive Officer of EDS, goes further and with characteristic vigour:

'The Internet ... is a market-space, a cost-free distribution channel, that allows companies to control the new commanding heights. The new Network Economy puts a trillion dollar's worth of technology – from network connections, processing power, memory and limitless databases – in the hands of anyone with a phone and a PC. This means that the end consumer, and the buyers and sellers, the traditional middlemen in every deal, are now empowered consumers. If they don't like what you have to offer at the price they want to pay, they're gone in the blink of an eye. They'll go where they can get it the way they want it because the Internet has placed the global commodity market right on their desktop.'

But even in the near perfect market of the Internet, people (including business people) remain people. And just because the supply chain can be automated by the Internet, it doesn't mean that the people operating it are automatons. Flesh and blood still lurk behind the suits and not every decision will be taken on strictly ratiocinative grounds. The Internet carries advertising just like traditional media do. Phrases such as 'I know their prices are a tad higher, I'm just happier with them' will still be heard. And that wonderful skunk instinct – which I talk about in Chapter 9 – should never be ignored. What is it? It is the capacity of some gifted human beings to smell a skunk when no skunk is in sight. 'It looks good on screen, but I wonder…' is the typical warning cry.

Business people buying from suppliers through the Net still need the reassurance and encouragement that only contact with the 'All' of the supplier can give.

Four

The RelModel at work

I T IS DIFFICULT, no it is impossible, to describe a business model without generalising. Generalising makes the model look neat and tidy, logical and sensible. It also gives it an aura of sweetness and light.

Life, of course, isn't like that and no great venture has even been accomplished by anyone, whether government, business or private individuals, without the sweetness turning sour at some point and even the light starting to flicker. However, if you tried to describe any new business programme only in terms of real life, then the description would never end. Human beings, each with a genome containing several trillion genes, most of which are at some time in conflict with each other, are themselves too complex to be reduced easily to tidiness, logic and holistic common sense.

You can apply the same stimuli to any number of those complicated entities and get in return the same number of responses, but all of them different. You can give any number of people and companies the same programme of action to follow and end up with as many different responses as the number of people and companies you began with. All of which is a good reason for *starting* with a programme that *does* have all those qualities, a programme that *is* tidy, logical and sensible. 'All-to-One', implemented via the RelModel, is all three.

Having voiced all those reservations, I now provide a case study that demonstrates a remarkably tidy, logical and sensible expression of 'All-to-One' principles!

British Airways (BA) adopted the 'All-to-One' philosophy in the late 1980s (I told you there was nothing new about 'All-to-One' except the name – it wasn't called that then) and carried it through with quite astonishing success in an atmosphere that for most of the time almost amounted to camaraderie. The reason is simple, and is a point I make elsewhere in connection with company culture: nothing substantial ever happens in a company, and certainly nothing happens smoothly and effectively, without the active backing and involvement of the Chief Executive. Let there be the slightest doubt about the commitment of the boss, and the doubters, worriers and trouble-makers will start to nit-pick ('you appear to have forgotten our agreement with the French, tut-tut' or even more discouraging 'we know what the boss really thinks of all this nonsense') and move into positions where their backs are covered. Not helpful.

So ... principle No. 1 for 'All-to-One': the CEO must be seen to be an enthusiastic part of the 'All'.

That was certainly the case at BA where Sir John King (later Lord King) and his successor, Sir Colin Marshall (later Lord Marshall), led from the front. Coffee cups rattled on tables several offices away when either of them made a point about the need for further acceleration of the 'All-to-One' programme. They were committed all right and the whole company knew it.

I can speak of British Airways and the programme with inside knowledge because I was part of it. The sad thing for me, as it has been for many others, is that having showed brilliantly how 'All-to-One' can work and having projected the benefits not only to consumers and staff but also to the bottom line, the company went pear-shaped. They did it and they undid it. Happily the years between doing it and undoing it sufficed to show what 'All-to-One' can achieve. This is how it happened – I can only give the outlines, partly from reasons of space, but they do accurately summarise what actually happened.

Level 1? Just!

Back in 1986, British Airways was vulnerable in the marketplace. It was losing money, it still bore the scars of state ownership, and it was still traumatised, not least because its release from state control had been delayed twice for political reasons. Consumers saw BA as cold, arrogant, uncaring, bureaucratic, class-ridden and patronising. It was making poor use of the technology available. It was unable to respond quickly and effectively to challenges, both those endemic to the industry (such as consumer peaks, changes in demand, fluctuating fuel prices, escalating costs of new aircraft) and those forced on it by competitors (such as price cutting, new services, better benefits). It was vulnerable to the apathy even hostility of third parties, most notably the travel agents. It was being bled by new entrants to the airline business, who through their core businesses and image had better access to consumers and a reputation that consumers found particularly attractive. (Laker, with his magnificently cut-price Atlantic flights, is only one example, although it happened to attract the most headlines.) It was outplayed by competitors, US airlines predominating, who had stronger networks and a more flexible infrastructure. BA had only just reached Level 1 of the RelModel!

Something had to be done. It was. The first step was the appointment of John King as boss – nothing good happens unless the boss is up to it. Then King did what every boss has to do – he appointed his eventual successor. The name: Colin Marshall.

Level 2 – here they come

Colin Marshall wasted no time. With his marketing team, he created a new master brand positioning for BA, supported by the key 'pillar' brands or 'service marks' that were targeted at particular consumer segments. Then there was the initiative to combine technology with consumer service and aim communications directly at the most valued consumers. He set up a four-tier relationship marketing strategy focused on the business executive passenger (at this stage the Executive Club stood at 38,000 members but was not used in any strategic way). No one knew who the best consumers were, except for a vague idea that they would include glamorous high-fliers with names like Joan Collins (only one of those unfortunately). In fact, and rather unglamorously, BA's best consumer at the time was the head of IT at Reuters who had a regular weekly meeting in New York. You wouldn't have guessed that just by guessing. You had to do some serious consumer information analysis.

So, with the consumer information it could now access, the marketing team was able to introduce differing service levels for each of the four tiers of the Executive Club (Premier, Gold, Silver and Blue). Membership of each tier depended on the individual's travel spend. These were the first steps in consumer segmentation and interaction that characterise Level 2 of the RelModel, targeting consumers by value, style and tone.

Achieving Level 3

Membership of the Executive Club was designed to encourage loyalty and profits by offering truly worthwhile benefits. Systems were set up that tracked all relevant travel bookings so that regular individual travellers could be recognised – and as a result well looked after by consumer service staff from the time they booked through to the end of their journey.

And so to Level 4

Thanks to the information gained from the tracking, resources could be targeted on the most regular and thus most valuable consumers. They received special attention whenever they travelled. They were encouraged by rewards and incentives to make more journeys by BA – on shorter internal trips instead of road or rail and on weekend breaks or family holidays.

Incentives were tiered so that the more you flew BA the more valuable the benefits you received. The very top tier offered benefits for those spending more than £25,000 a year. These benefits included late check-ins (every business person's dream), 'your baggage in the crew hold' to save you time and hassle on arrival, and 24-hour access to the BA country manager – so 'wherever in the world you were, you had direct person-to-person contact with the individual with real power to help'.

A lively communications programme, based principally on personally addressed and therefore very direct mail, kept high-value business travellers up to date with the benefits on offer to them. It also kept them *au courant* with what was going on inside the airline – airlines are interesting entities, especially for those who fly them regularly. The results of the mailings were carefully analysed to check that the targets had been reached and the overall objectives attained. The information helped to push the company up the learning curve.

BA staff were the decisive element in the whole programme. Any member of staff, with one unconsidered remark to a consumer, one piece of inefficiency or thoughtlessness, had the power to unravel anything achieved by the programme. The staff, all of them, were well aware of their responsibilities and were involved with management from the start. A worldwide communications programme addressed everyone in the enterprise, the *extended* enterprise – because the programme talked with the staff of other airlines, for instance handling staff acting on behalf of BA. To help motivate the people delivering the service, the top-rating TV programme *Cheers* was used to get the message across (it was one of my favourites and I expect one of yours at the time). The tag line for the intro to *Cheers* was 'A place where everyone knows your name'. This was used as a tag line for the programme. Just as at the corner shop, you would feel welcome at BA, and be treated as an individual, with your preferred seat and your usual gin and tonic ready waiting for you.

The programme also targeted travel agents, the people who held power of 'yes and no' over ticket sales. The effectiveness of the communications and the consumer service approach was measured through control groups.

Level 5 and 'All-to-One'

With all the consumer information now at its disposal, the airline could be increasingly selective in the treatment of consumers. No one was short-changed, everyone was treated to the highest possible degree of service – for the extra reason that everyone had the capacity to become a high-value consumer. However, those consumers who had already reached that status were given special treatment. When upgrades to First Class were available, the high-value consumer was given priority. In-flight service was personalised ('Good morning, Mr Robinson, we've got one of your favourites on the menu today'). In the unhappy event of overbooking, the high-value consumer was the last to be off-loaded. (Overbooking is genuinely unavoidable in airline operations if sensible economics and therefore sensible pricing is to be maintained.) For the first time BA was able to differentiate and recognise its most valuable consumers.

The results were impressive. At the end of 18 months, membership of the Executive Club had doubled and subscriptions were up by a further 50 per cent. The control group showed an increase in travelling revenue of 24 per cent for those targeted by the communications plan.

The second tier within the Gold Card membership showed a 15 per cent increase in revenue over and above that averaged for the group overall, attributable to the desire to maintain sufficient travel to qualify for this card and its benefits. Responses for individual mailing campaigns were high and reached 33 per cent in some cases, a very satisfactory percentage.

The quick recovery of BA after the Libyan crisis was attributed to its use of the database to keep and then encourage its high-value consumers to travel.

Branding

With awareness – and respect – for its major brand already assured, the airline buttressed it still further by introducing a range of 'pillar' brands. One of these, Club World, focused on the glamour and drama of business life at 30,000 feet, offering every business traveller the mystique of belonging to an exclusive club where million-dollar deals, boardroom bust-ups and major decisions were everyday events. By massaging the business consumer's self-esteem, Club World really took off. It had the effect of convincing this important consumer segment that they were particularly valued by the airline, which understood their special needs and were determined and able to satisfy them.

The airline took the same approach with Club Europe. Here the travellers were more time-conscious and less concerned with the creature comforts appropriate to a long-haul flight. The time-conscious aspect of Club Europe was paralleled by a UK domestic service branded the Super Shuttle. This offered flights at regular intervals and guaranteed a seat for anyone who turned up, enforcing the guarantee with a back-up aircraft – even if only one passenger needed it! The Super Shuttle showed the airline's commitment to meeting the real needs of business.

'All-to-One' consolidates

The company re-organised itself to focus on the consumer. Pilots and cabin crew, previously running an empire on their own, now considered themselves part of marketing. The old military terms (they still said 'Engage the doors') was jettisoned for more consumer-friendly and understandable language. Pilots were no longer running an operation. They were part of the service, providing the comfort feeling, the reassuring 'I'm in control part' of the consumers' experience – and an integral part of the brand.

BA consolidated further by setting up a Brands Team and a Distribution Task Force to carry out programmes linked to the overall strategy but without the distraction of operational day-to-day business responsibilities.

Enterprise-wide data and systems support

The BABS (British Airways Business System) was enterprise-wide and covered the full global operation. It held information on all travel-agent bookings, passenger tickets, flights and so forth. All passenger interactions could be monitored. This information was fully utilised for the first time. It was downloaded to a Consumer Marketing Database System and could be accessed by those responsible for the delivery and tracking of marketing communications to consumers. The information they acquired as a result was fed back to BABS.

Understanding the consumer

The processes by which consumers made their decision to fly with this or that airline and the influences that helped govern them were well understood. Programmes were set up to target such key 'influences' as executive secretaries. Frequent, very high-value travellers were given the British Airways Gold Card, which offered important privileges, such as priorities in booking, luxury facilities at the airports and in-flight VIP treatment.

A children's programme – branded as SkyFlyers – aimed at creating what is unkindly called 'parent pester pressure'. Children were made aware of the goodies offered by BA to them, provided only that someone in their family flew with the airline.

The people

The culture created was passionate for success – that's the only phrase! Teamwork was taken for granted, success was everyone's responsibility and the consumer ruled the roost.

The airline introduced a series of schemes designed to enhance the performance and hence the careers of every one in the airline. Among them were the famous 'Putting People First' campaign and the 'Day in the Life' programmes. These programmes were all about culture change on an enterprise scale. Everyone in the company went on them, everyone. It was a huge investment and sent out clear messages to all employees: BA was changing ... the leadership was highly committed and was putting big money behind it. Everything was new, the competitive edge was instilled by focusing on the competition and on the consumer. 'Putting People First' was all about recognising that if your people were not happy they would not be giving the best to consumers. The message certainly got across and 'Putting People First' was a message to everyone – it was everyone's responsibility. Yes, you! You had to take heed and be seen putting your colleagues first, to 'walk the talk'.

It certainly worked. 'Putting People First' was the initial programme and was followed by more. 'More' is very important. Culture development is not a one-shot deal – it is on-going. As one senior executive at the time put it in a familiar but always effective simile: an organisation is like a super tanker ... it takes time to turn it around. You need to set it off in the right direction, but you have to keep directing it, otherwise the rocks will be waiting ('be guided by the rudder or punished by the rocks!').

The 'Day in the Life' follow-up was designed to show people in the organisation what other BA people did – engineers, aircraft cleaners, call centre representatives, salespeople on the road, operations supervisors in Delhi, announcers in Chicago, everybody everywhere. It was all about re-inforcing the team spirit, emphasising the value of every role and projecting one face to the consumer.

There were other cultural and people-related programmes. One was 'Young Professionals' which sponsored 12 entrepreneurial mid-twenties graduates to roam the departments, before setting up and implementing new and innovative projects, shaking out the cobwebs of pre-privatisation days, offering fresh insights, breathing new ideas and always challenging the traditional. As you can imagine, they were not always popular but they demonstrated a new desire to take risks and provided the momentum to change.

And there was renewed focus on who precisely the competitors were (called the 'enemy' for short – nothing gives an organisation more cohesion, *esprit de corps* and the determination to succeed as an outside enemy).

Innovation and risk

There was plenty of both, the classic instance being the huge investment in the Galileo reservations system where the risk was that the partners in Galileo were, until recently, competitors – and might become so again.

Integrated consumer service

The actual consumer experience was tied into the data. Personal preferences were noted and acted on to achieve an exceptional level of consumer care. BA knew which passengers wanted vegetarian meals, who preferred aisle seats (or window seats), who liked what drink. People who complained had their complaints sorted and the points raised added to the database.

Good internal communication

People in the airline were kept continually up to speed with developments and proposals. The usual array of internal media was deployed, but as always the key to good internal communications is 'management walking about' to adapt Tom Peters' great phrase. People knew who their leaders were and respected and liked them. Lord King, Sir Colin Marshall, Gordon Dunlop, Nick Georgiades, Mike Levin all provided strong leadership direction and drive. They fought for the airline in its relationships with government and with other airlines, and they gave staff the pre-eminence that human beings expect, and like when they get it. They supported the staff in everything they did. It was 'inverted pyramid' management at its best. The campaign 'Putting People First' included staff as well as passengers!

For me, as a young executive taking everything in, this period was a great learning experience – don't get me wrong, I did my bit with ideas, drive and so on (I was actually one of those annoying know-better YPs I talked about earlier) but I was able to get around the whole airline and see all of the initiatives in place and I was particularly proud to be involved with the introduction of the first Gold Card in any of the service industries. Technology linked to service, linked to brand, linked to consumer focus, linked to culture and people focus and not forgetting the competition – these were the hallmarks of the BA transformation from redundant, demoralised, state-owned disaster to a flourishing, combative, confident, trailblazing travel industry revolutionary. This is really the creation of 'All-to-One' and shows it can be done.

The story must end on a low note. BA seems, at least until recently, to have forgotten its attachment to 'All-to-One' principles and its RelModel competencies. Instead cost reductions began to take priority, the 'All-to-One' culture we all thought endemic in the airline began to fade, and with it the enthusiasm and cooperation of the staff. You can build a winning culture and brand image over years and lose it overnight. If you let the culture deteriorate, and with it the passion of your workforce to deliver exceptional service, then the whole thing fails. It shows in the bottom line. It shows in the side issues too. Take the tail-fin fiasco. That wouldn't have happened in the glory days. For those lucky enough to have missed the on-going shambles, here is a very quick recap.

Sometime during the middle 1990s, the new management at BA had become concerned that 60 per cent of their passengers were non-British (if you're the world's favourite airline, what else can you expect?). They were even more concerned when low-cost airlines began to eat at their leisure travel business. One reason perhaps was 'the flag'. It's too British. So the call went out: let's have a Master Brand Repositioning Plan – forgetting that the 60 per cent of the foreigner segment had chosen to fly with BA and its traditional design. They wanted to keep the global brand feel, but to aspire to something 'less formal, and more flexible, catering more to our consumers' individual needs' in the words of the then Chief Executive. Noble aims, but one of the ways they chose to achieve them was to 'turn the fleet into a flying gallery – one of the world's largest art commissions' to quote the Chief Executive again. This is not what airlines are about. The new livery upset existing consumers (Prime Minister Margaret Thatcher, when shown a model of a new liveried aircraft, covered up its most offending part – the art on the tail-fin). It also failed to appeal to the right numbers of new ones. The look of the livery with its conflict between the name and the 'international art' was confusing, as if the professional adviser you liked and respected suddenly turned up for a meeting in flowery Bermuda shorts. The image did not stem, as it should have done, from the true character of the airline, its staff and its culture. It was not 'All-to-One'. It was a disaster – rather like BA's old slogan 'We'll take more care of you' and British Rail's 'We're getting there', both of which flew in the face of obvious reality.

The master Brand Repositioning Programme was carried out alongside other 'non-All-to-One' *faux pas*. Everyone knew at the time about the poor employee management, the pilot show-downs, the cabin crew disputes and so forth. The people who make the airline work are the brand ambassadors. When they are not treated with care, how can you expect them to treat the consumers with care. More: in the summer of 1996 Egon Ronay slated the BA Shuttle breakfasts; then came the long saga of the American Airline alliance where competitive advantage came first and the consumer a poor second; meantime the on-going battle with Virgin rumbled into the legal arena with more press acres and TV aeons of negative impact on the BA caring image. Staff morale continued to tumble, so did the share price, those who could be bothered even queried BA's proud claim to be 'the world's favourite airline'.

In 1997 a senior executive was quoted as saying 'The day British Airways starts losing its reputation is the day it starts losing money'. Well said.

How CarPlus won my vote at RelModel Level 5

Let's now look at how a company, on reaching RelModel Level 5, could be perceived by the consumer. The following is a diary extract of a consumer buying a new car. While this is fictional, it shows what companies could achieve if they apply 'All-to-One'. For sake of argument, we have called the car manufacturer 'CarPlus'.

Quick introduction to CarPlus

The consumer starts out life as a prospect for a brand. CarPlus will spend at least 60 per cent of its marketing budget to conquest a prospect. The shopping-phase part of the decision process is either traditional or conducted online. Interesting then that CarPlus has the highest number of consumers in the automotive industry who are Internet users. To make the prospect's life easier the Internet site is connected to an interactive call centre that in turn records the prospect's response to a press ad or a direct mail piece or an e-mail (note the 'All-to-One' type media mix). Alternatively any information requests that generate from the prospect visiting CarPlus's website are automatically recorded for follow-up purposes by CarPlus and its dealer network. So prospects can in effect select their own communication channel and decide how they want to be spoken to and when. Convenience and accessibility are key, 'All-to-One' the guiding philosophy. So here comes the story of:

CarPlus and the delighted consumer

Sunday Morning

Just seen my next car in this week's *Sunday Times* – a CarPlus Convertible. The ad said to ring an 0800 number or access the website (Level 3?). I chose the call centre and booked a test drive for the following weekend – my wife's birthday. I'd been thinking of taking her down to the coast. CarPlus surprise me by saying, yes, the car's yours for 24 hours, and will be delivered to my home at a time to suit. The call centre say that it will create a test drive page for me on its website. I spend time over the following week exploring the site and even building my 'ideal CarPlus convertible'. The site feeds back all the finance information I asked for, even giving me an online quote for my old BMW as part exchange!

Next Saturday

The car arrives as planned ... bunch of flowers in the front seat for my wife (Level 5!). They must have checked her birthday from the information I gave the call centre regarding temporary insurance cover. The flowers came through a local florist – who offer me a 15 per cent discount on my next order. Test drive is great. We like the car.

Sunday Morning

CarPlus pick up the car from my home. Within one hour the call centre rings to ask if we enjoyed the test drive, did my wife enjoy her birthday, would we like to think of buying from CarPlus. No hard sell, but a suggestion to revisit the website.

Wednesday

My wife hasn't stopped talking about the test drive. I ring the call centre, agree the spec and price, place the order and agree a delivery date. I can have the car delivered or pick it up from my local dealer. I decide to go to the dealer as I need to know where to go for a service. 'That's no problem', says the call centre, 'in future your car can be picked up from either your home or where you work when it's due for service'. (We're definitely on Level 5 now – feels good too.) The call centre tell me later that day that they have set up my own home page to make it easier to 'talk to CarPlus'. All delivery details of the car, price, less part exchange, insurance, and delivery date are confirmed online. I even have my own dedicated Consumer Service Assistant in case I need someone to talk to!

Friday

I go to pick my car up from the local dealership. It's ready as planned according to the e-mail schedule received last week. I'm introduced to my Consumer Service Assistant. Then get in the car to find an invitation for an on-the-house meal at the local French restaurant plus a bottle of champagne courtesy of the dealer and my local wine store (with a special case offer as a welcome to CarPlus's Wine Club).

When I get home I find my CarPlus home page full of special offers that appeal to both of us, together and separately. The call centre calls a week later to ask: 'Was everything OK with both the car and the dealer?' And would I mind answering some more questions as part of their research programme.

CarPlus now have a full and accurate view of my first month as a consumer!

Six months later

My first service is due. My Consumer Service Assistant called to arrange for the car to be picked up from my house. It is – and in its place I have a fully accessorised convertible to use as a courtesy car.

I like the wind-deflector device. I ring the call centre and ask them to arrange for one to be fitted to the car during the service. I use my CarPlus credit card for the transaction. The points I have been earning since I applied for my card have paid for the wind deflector. The car returns with details on the fascia-panel readout about my next service and a new service offered by the dealership – overnight car repairs and valet service. I glance at my consumer home page that night, to find they have just launched a web-based insurance locator programme. Within 90 seconds we have a quote for our holiday which starts on Friday. (If this is Level 5, give me more of it.)

Year 1

What a year! We are now part of a CarPlus Consumer Management Programme. It offers all kinds of web and WAP-enabled products and services. One result: I've transferred my bank accounts to the CarPlus Net Saver. It has a tie-up with my credit card and in effect offers me a discount on my next CarPlus purchase. I receive an online magazine each quarter featuring special deals on servicing and accessories. We've just decided to go on a touring holiday this year with my brother and his wife. He has a CarPlus too, bought on my recommendation two months ago. CarPlus Holiday Services are arranging all our travel and hotel accommodation. Not bad for a car manufacturer!

Boo.com

Why Boo bombed and Wrangler succeeds

L IKE YESTERDAY, or so it seemed, but actually as far back as 1998, two Swedish entrepreneurs had this great idea: 'let's build the first truly global Internet retailer of fashion sportswear, with offices in London's Carnaby Street plus New York, Munich, Paris and, of course, Stockholm and let's call it Boo.com.' They couldn't go wrong. They had already built up and sold an online bookseller in Sweden. That worked. For their next venture they chose a field where tastes are global, margins high, consumers young, wired up and 'don't bother us with details like price'. They had 300 staff, the brightest of the bright. They were backed by Goldman Sachs, JP Morgan, Benetton and other big names. Eighteen months and £85 million or so later, they went bust.

The excuses are familiar: outgoings not controlled (Concorde flights to the USA don't come cheap); website too high-tech (you could dress a model in your chosen gear); day-to-day management under par; they tried to move too quickly too soon.

Yes, yes, yes and yes. But the company had no life outside the Internet, company and consumers had no real contact with each other. Could those two facts have been contributory to the bankruptcy? Definitely yes.

Moral: dotcom companies cannot buck the laws of economics and the fundamentals of marketing. 'All-to-One' will always beat one-to-one.

Why the Wrangler way works

Wrangler operates in the market now abandoned by Boo.com, but with the benefit of an established brand (aren't brands wonderful?). Wrangler's e-commerce venture is working superbly.

Case study (continued)

Two obvious advantages contribute to the success:

❏ The website is fun, simple to understand, easy to access.

❏ The site is highly interactive, for instance consumers can chat with each other.

But the key reasons are the 'All-to-One' reasons:

❏ The site links to the printed catalogue and in-store marketing themes.

❏ Site visitors are encouraged to go to a real retail point of purchase – and are told where the nearest one is.

❏ Retailers are delighted with the referrals ...

❏ ... and they get updated on the latest marketing schemes, etc. through an Intranet.

Call it 'All-to-One' if you like. Wrangler calls it common sense. Call it what you like. It works.

Five

Closer to the consumer via RelTechnics

'Some 70% of delivering consumer value is about making them feel like a human being. This is the most profoundly simple idea that everyone in the consumer arena tends to miss.'

John McKean,
Executive Director for the Center for Information Based Competition, Ohio

MARKETING IS VERY simple, at least it is in principle, though to read some marketing books or attend some marketing courses you'd think even the principle was complex and difficult. But the principle really is simple – it is all about understanding the consumers in the marketplace, turning them into *your* consumers and then maximising the lifetime value of those consumers to your organisation.

Let me expand on the diagram a little. It begins by telling you to understand your consumers. But before you can understand them, you have to get close to them, as close as possible. To do that, you need to know them, which means that you must tap as many sources of information about them as possible. Some of the sources will be in the public domain, such as those providing basic demographic data, some you'll have to pay for, such as specially commissioned research, some you will already hold in databases or in the minds of your people – at which point danger cones are hoisted. Information about

Marketing is very simple

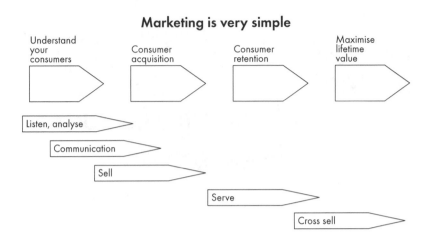

consumers held in your people's minds should be committed now to some kind of easily accessible storage. You can hardly overestimate the importance of making all the information held within a company open and available for everyone in the company to use. Most marketing people even those of only a few years standing can relate horror stories of commissioning expensive new research, which turns out to be simply a duplication of research carried out a month or two previously by another department of the same company. So important is this sharing of data company-wide that I have covered it at length in Chapter 10.

It really is essential to gather consumer information from as many different sources as possible. The more you do that, the more likely it is that you'll end up with a rounded picture of your prospective consumers and hence more likely to understand their needs and wants.

By the way, I use two words – needs and wants. I do that because I think it helps our understanding of consumers to distinguish between those product categories which are by any modern standards vital to life – food, clothing, warmth, health and education – and those which add to the amenities of life – transport, labour-saving equipment, cosmetics, entertainment, holidays and the like.

So, you have to get close to your consumers, as close as possible, understand them, direct at each one of them all the good and appropriate benefits your company has to offer, communicate with each one of them in all the ways open to you, find out what each one wants or needs or both, then provide it for them. Do all that and you'll find that consumers stay with you for life, and you'll find it easier to acquire new consumers.

That's the principle. What about the detail, because that's where the real work lies.

I've designed a number of simple techniques, call them tools if you like, that should help you get on top of the detail. Their aim is to help you achieve that target of lifetime relationships with consumers – which is the most profitable relationship. They've certainly worked and are working for me.

So, let's always look at the world from the perspective of the consumer in every way and for every step of the way. If you are closer to the consumers in the market and to your own consumers, you will win. If your competitors are closer, then they will win.

I have called this range of techniques – 'RelTechnics' – short, as you've guessed, for relationship techniques. RelTechnics consists of a series of five 'models': the consumer lifestyle model; the consumer decision-making model; the consumer buying process model; the consumer transaction model and the consumer retention/defection model. These five techniques will enhance your relationships with the consumers in the market. I recommend that as you go through these different RelTechnics, you refer to John Caswell's pull-out 'All-to-One' Journey Map at the back of the book.

People often think, mistakenly, that you can only have relationships with people who have already signed up to your products or services. These techniques will show how to develop relationships with people who have not signed up, and create that 'emotion bond' which will link them with you and your brand and turn them into your consumers. It is not simply about how they understand and feel about you. It is also how you understand and see them.

By implementing these RelTechnics, you will find that you are getting closer to all consumers and automatically developing an integrated 'All-to-One' marketing programme complete from initial strategy through to final execution.

RelTechnic 1: consumer lifestyle model

Your first step is to create a lifestyle model of the consumer in the market that concerns you.

Apart from exceptional circumstances — at a sale for instance where an otherwise unacceptable product or brand is offered at an irresistibly low price — consumers will only buy products that fit their lifestyles, as perceived by them. In other words, they buy on emotion, on an emotional link between their lifestyle and the product or service. The link could have, almost certainly will have, a stiffening of fact. People don't want to think they are being conned by what they buy, or, even more, do they want other people to think they are being conned. People do need their purchase to be justified by factual, technical arguments. But the more powerful arguments are emotional.

When the moment of truth comes and money is about to change hands, people choose this product rather than that one because this product helps them to feel safer, prouder, more highly thought of. It fits in better with their idea of themselves, with their lifestyle. That one doesn't, which is why brands have always scored over commodities (and why, while we're about it, some brands have beaten others into the undergrowth). Commodities can only make factual promises. Brands add the all-important emotional overtones. Sainsbury's economy packs with their austere monochrome design contain simply 'economy porridge oats' or 'economy baked beans' or 'economy sliced peaches'. To a hungry castaway on a desert island that list of plain foods would sound like bliss. To a consumer in a rich western-style society, they sound boring, sterile and third best. Compare them with the rich imagery, the history, the advertising echoes stretching back down the years plus all those 'we are your friends' overtones of 'Scott's Porridge Oats', 'Heinz Baked Beans' and

'Del Monte Peaches'. The fact is that when you buy a brand you don't just buy a product, you buy an emotional experience. I can't write the word Heinz without recalling those wonderful childhood teatimes on a winter Saturday afternoon with the football results coming in on the telly – not to mention so many other happy experiences of the brand over the years. In short, the brand chimes with my lifestyle, every relevant part of it. I don't get that with Sainsbury's economy baked beans – although groups buying on price might. I have a relationship with Heinz, one of lifetime value to both of us, though how much that is worth to Heinz in hard cash only they will know. I don't keep count. All of us have relationships of varying degrees of intensity with brands. You will have your favourites, either for yourself or for your children.

Brands have and always will have the key to sales and profit. Even a pure Internet tool such as a search engine will succeed on the emotion-bond it creates with a consumer, the level of trust it achieves and the reputation for reliability. Brands are another example of 'All-to-One' in action. On a one-to-one test with Heinz, just the beans against the beans, Sainsbury's economy would probably do well. Throw onto the scales the weight of the Heinz image nourished by advertising, promotions, word of mouth and everyday experience of the taste, and there is no contest (unless the consumer happens to be one of the low-price-first stalwarts). For most people, that 'All-to-One' emotional extra tips the balance decisively. And so with every other brand on the market. This, of course, is why brands will always command a premium price. They call to witness all the attributes of the product, all the aspects of its history, all the past and present advertising and promotion, all the word of mouth, and they present all that to each and every individual who is about to choose between the branded product and its non-branded alternative. And because of the trust that has been built up over the years between brand and consumer, the images called up are believed, taken for granted as real. In effect, they say to the individual: we are part of your lifestyle.

To reach the position where your brands are a trusted part of people's lifestyle, where consumers in the marketplace become your consumers, you must track the lifestyle, learn all you can about the habits, interests, hobbies, moods and buying modes (the lifestyle litany changes only its words not its significance).

Your consumer lifestyle model should include as foundation all the usual demographic information, age, gender, marital status, occupation, etc. With these you need to put the unique lifestyle data which can be grouped under three main headings: habits, attitudes and interests, with an almost endless list of subheads, some of which can be entered under more than one heading. These subheads can include hopes, fears, likes and dislikes, leisure, work, family, colleagues, hobbies, sport (spectator or player), health and fitness, clubs and societies, clothes, food, drink, politics, the environment, religion.

You should also track their typical daily routine: what time does she get up; how far does she travel to work; what relationships does she have at work (what does she think of the boss?); are the systems always crashing; what does she have for lunch; what time does she finish; when does she pop to the shops; which friends does she meet in the evening; how much time does she spend playing tennis or whatever, or at the cinema/theatre, etc.

Search through the files for relevant research information. So much research is done and then filed away under lock and key never to see the light of day let alone the eyes of the people who could make good use of it. All relevant research should be made available throughout the organisation. Directors, operations people, consumer service teams, the lot should have sight of it. Simply doing that will help generate a culture of being close to consumers and close to the market.

Best of all, the once hidden information can join all other information to help create true-to-life 'portraits' of the relevant target market.

How? Paint a verbal picture of the members of your target groups, give them real names, a personality, get someone to draw them, or simply cut out photographs from magazines and newspapers that resemble them, create stories and life histories, make lists of their interests, hobbies, favourite sports, make tape recordings of characteristic conversations, anything to make your target group come alive in your mind and in the minds of your team. This again is the 'All-to-One' concept at work but from a different angle. This time all the information concerning the prospect is directed at the company, and especially those people directly responsible for the marketing. The net result is to highlight the complexity of the 'ordinary' human beings you are trying to influence.

Imaginative input of this kind brings the target audience to life in your offices and in your internal presentations, and above all in the minds of those responsible for planning the marketing strategies and carrying them out. It reminds everyone again that marketing is about people and that the statistics are only a short-hand way of referring to real people, and it you're not careful a misleading way.

It also makes for more entertaining, more memorable, more effective presentations. As such they are useful aids to career advancement, though such thoughts would not be present in your mind, would they?

Everyone should be exposed to these 'All-to-One' presentations. After all, everyone in the organisation in one way or another has a role to play, and not simply the service and operational teams, though, of course, their involvement is critical because it is they who will be seeing, dealing closely with your target groups.

Quite often you don't need to have real paid-for research. You can use your own experience and that of your company. It helps though to have the real thing, and gives you more credibility at those important board room presentations. Internal workshops with the people who actually meet consumers and potential consumers would be very useful. You can later back it up with independent research. The internal workshops will help in defining consumer needs and hence your specific research needs, whether they call for formal quantifiable research with lengthy questionnaires or simply group discussions or even single-person interviews. Those last two are useful for pinpointing the underlying needs and priorities of your consumer groups.

So the first technique for getting closer to consumers is the one that helps you and all the people in your organisation understand consumers' lifestyle and gain a clear idea of who the target consumers are.

I have created a template for you to consider when pinpointing your consumer groups and creating your consumer lifestyle profiles (below). I hope you find it useful. Anyway, have a go and involve your people. Filling in templates is always a valuable and fun part of the 'All-to-One' experience.

Consumer Lifestyle Model — Profile Template

1. Who are they?

Demographic _____   Socio-demographic grouping _____

Sex _____   Age _____   Lifestage _____

Employment _____   Geographic boundaries _____

Location type _____   Family status _____

Housing _____   Other _____

2. What do they do?

Habits _____   Day in the life_____

Work _____ Travel _____   Leisure _____

Shopping _____   Health _____

Eating   _____   Relationships _____

Groups _____

3. How do they feel?

Attitudes _____

Emotions _____

Modes_____   Moods_____

Loyalty_____

Brands_____

The consumer lifestyle profiles will determine how you attract consumers and present your product or service. The timing, the place, the choice of media will all be determined by your target consumers' behaviour. Track their behaviour and track your communications. Your findings will determine when the prospects would be receptive to certain messages and when they won't. Most people lead double lives of a sort. Someone may be an office worker during the day, when he or she is responsive to certain kinds of messages expressed in a certain way in certain kinds of media. In the evening and at weekends, that same person becomes a leisure person, responsive to different messages, expressed in different ways in different media. Or take the executive entitled to a company car. Anyone trying to promote their model would have to take into account not only the proposed business use, but the leisure use too, with the emphasis weighed heavily on the latter. The messages, the timing and media would have to cover both sets of requirements.

RelTechnic 2: consumer decision-making model

Once you have decided upon your consumer groups, the next level of preparation is to understand how consumers make their decisions, what influences them, who influences them, where do they get their information from, what are their needs and why those particular needs, what are their priorities. All this helps you understand the media you should be using to reach them. Some companies, not just toy manufacturers, have understood that to get at mum's purse you have to market to her kids (other examples are breakfast food manufacturers – Kellogg show how it should be done – just think of the Rice Krispies commercials among many similar products). Other companies have realised that to sell to kids you have to get their mums to give clearance. The classic example today of mum-as-censor is in the selling of home computers to children. In one of AOL's major TV campaigns in the UK, a Julie Andrews lookalike (she doesn't sing though) reassures the newly wired-up boy that everything about the Internet is easy to operate and are as good as free – the boy had been having nightmares about the phone bill. The real target of the wholesome Julie-clone is the mother – your child is safe with us. This is one of a range of ads in a great campaign. On an even more ambitious scale, those in the USA who are trying to promote soccer are targeting the kids, getting them to punt the round ball about on any spare piece of grass or concrete. The idea is that the mums and dads will follow their kids, and a whole new fan-base is created.

British Airways (BA) created the Executive Secretary International, the target being, not executive secretaries who might fly on business, but those secretaries who booked tickets for those who did fly on business – the bosses. The bosses, or rather the bosses' wallets, were reached through their secretaries. Likewise, BA created the kiddies club so that when the busy international executive flies home he or she is faced by eager children pulling on the emotional strings and asking for the BA children's pack they'd heard of. 'What, you haven't got one?' Next time you will.

The car industry on the other hand has not made the connection between fleet sales and domestic usage. Ostensibly, the car is bought for business use. The fact is that the car is probably used just as much for domestic use. So who decides the specification? Who says 'We'll have a saloon or an estate car or a people carrier?' Who makes the final buying decision? Or, more realistically, who has the greatest influence on the final buying decision? The answer is probably a joint decision between company, husband and wife, but the requirements of each have to be met. Otherwise, no sale. And not just no sale now, but no sale with that family for the future. The car the parents have and their experience of it are powerful conditioners in the car-buying decisions of their children. There really are generations of people who have bought nothing but Fords. Others swear by BMW. Family loyalty is not to be downplayed.

Similar down-the-generation buying occurs in the vacation business. Any company selling vacations had better make sure that the children are included in the persuasion loop. 'That wonderful time we had at Benidorm in that really nice hotel' will remain a vivid colour image in the minds of young children as they grow up until the day comes when they have to decide where to take *their* young family. Benidorm and that very nice hotel will top the list of choices

An example of the factors influencing the business traveller

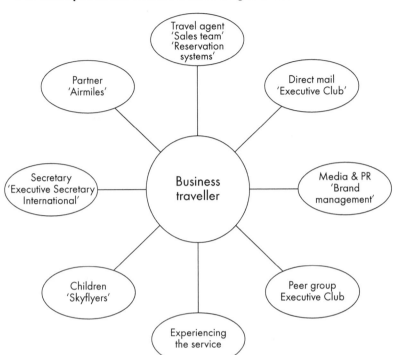

and will for years to come. Many families, like migrating birds, fly to the same spot for their holidays for decades!

What these examples tell us, and there are myriad more, is that many more people influence purchases than actually hand over the money. They also tell us that today's buying decisions can depend on buying decisions made many years earlier. They also tell us that people who apparently have no say on what is bought (children for example) are in fact the best long-term prospects.

Your consumer decision-making model has to take into account that far-reaching fact. The diagram above, for example, shows a decision-making model for the business traveller which does take account of it.

RelTechnic 3: consumer buying process model

This model looks at the series of steps an individual takes in buying a product or service (Figure 5.4). There is a different series for each product category, so it is important to map out and understand the steps the consumer groups have to take in your industry in order to buy your products or your competitors' products. If you understand those steps, you can track the consumers with your messages, and make sure you stay with them at all stages.

The questions to ask yourself are:

1. How do your consumers become aware?

2. How do consumers get hold of information?

3. What information do they want at which stage?

4. When do they go looking for it?

5. How do they go looking for it?

6. Do they get the right quality of information?

7. Is your competitors' information in a better format?

8. Is the information easily accessible?

9. How is that information tailored to the individual needs?

10. Plus the usual etceteras – those questions with very precise relevance to your company.

Take a typical holiday decision. There is any number of different routes, but they could be categorised under F for family and YS for young and single.

F for family first:

1. Christmas: family get-together. When the turkey and the other goodies have subsided, conversation turns to the future, to next year and to next year's holidays. Everyone has their say. In some cases, photographs from last year may be produced. Someone says: What about Turkey?

2. January: the sales may be disappointing, the weather appalling, but the holiday ads are blooming on the box and everywhere else. The younger son has explored the web and discovered some wonderful places to go.

3. February: the brochures start to arrive, are passed round and tentative decisions made on destination. Last year's success makes Benidorm – or wherever – still favourite. Mum hears holiday ad on the radio. It makes Hawaii seem feasible.

4. March: coffee-break/lunch-time/over-a-drink conversations cover the attractions of Benidorm alternatives. The papers carry even more holiday supplements. How about Florida?

5. April: the first bargains start to appear in the advertising. Suddenly Benidorm starts to seem pricey. Dad goes into travel agent and gets more ideas and more brochures. Someone says that the Italian Riviera is just as nice as the French version. But what about all those amazing offers for touring holidays in the Scottish Highlands? Yes, but would the kids enjoy that? And sun? Older son comes home from school with tales of snorkelling holidays off Crete.

6. May: decision time – inertia wins. Benidorm it is. It was a joint decision. No one came up with a better idea. The brochure was as good as ever. Main point was they enjoyed it last year.

YS for young and single:

1. September the year before: everyone's talking about the superb time they've just had in Crete. YS, who didn't go, makes a mental note.

2. Christmas: great time, next year's holiday rates not a mention.

3. January: can't avoid the holiday ads on the box, in the papers.

4. February: talks to friends (plural) or perhaps friend (singular) about going somewhere different this year. Friend produces brochure, and says the sailing and the diving are both good off Cornwall.

Consumer decision-making process

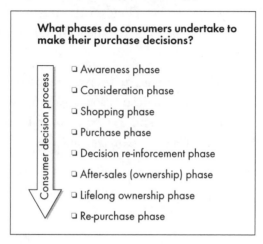

5. March: into the travel agencies. Nothing excites. Keeps on talking.

6. April: Tried the web. Found a club offering sailing/diving holidays all round the Mediterranean. Conversation about holiday plans now more focused.

7. May: The web turns up trumps with a sailing/diving holiday in the Red Sea. That's it.

RelModel 4: consumer transaction model

Once consumers have made their decision to buy, they have to decide how, where and when to close the deal – an activity I call 'the transaction'. This apparently simple decision is at the mercy of an army of variables. You should know which of the variables is the most likely to be the final persuader and be in a position to profit from it at the expense of your competitors. This is part of your distribution strategy – the right time the right place. The use of technology can help, for example the ATM (hole-in-the-wall cash dispenser) and the ability to do transactions over the phone. When you're first in your industry to offer a new transaction route that suits the convenience of your target group, you'll make a killing.

There is a range of transaction possibilities:

❏ Cash on the nail from the wallet or purse.

❏ Just wait a minute while I go to the cash till.

❏ Debit my account and I'll settle later by cheque or cash.

❏ Cheque through the post.

❏ Credit card at the point of purchase.

❏ Credit card on the phone.

❏ Credit card on the web.

❏ Credit card by post.

❏ Would you like to apply for our company credit card? It's only a formality.

❏ Nothing to pay till next year.

❏ Part-exchange.

❏ Barter (best for private deals, don't try it at the supermarket).

❏ Deferred terms with direct debit payments.

❏ Join the club – every member pays something every week and one member per week gets the products ordered (eventually everyone gets what they ordered).

None of them are new, though some may not be widely used in your industry, if so you're in with a chance. None of them in isolation has any particular advantage over the other. The choice depends on the circumstances of the moment and above all on the feelings of the consumer. You have to find out what those feelings are. When you do, you can provide the most favoured transaction arrangement – and knock competitors out of the bidding.

The consumer transaction model empowers you to jump way ahead of your competition. Your knowledge and understanding of the consumer's lifestyle and the steps the consumer takes in order to reach a decision will also help you understand what would be the best transaction route for that consumer and for you.

Here is an imaginary example of what I am getting at:

Let's say, for example, that only you can offer or had thought of offering deferred terms and let's also assume that your consumer groups tell you that this particular purchase (perhaps a holiday) always seems to set off a minor financial cash-flow crisis. Your approach is simple. You alert prospective consumers to the happy fact that they can now make their purchase on deferred terms. No one else is offering that method of payment, but 'you know how convenient it will be to you'. That kind of benefit goes straight to the pocket and is immediately noted in the heart. 'Here is a supplier who really understands.'

And here's a real example:

EasyJet, one of the UK's most successful bargain-flight operators, has persuaded all its consumers to book on the Internet and pay by credit card. By having the transaction completed through the Internet, EasyJet saves a pile of money, which it shares with its consumers. It also enhances its reputation as a modern, no-nonsense carrier.

'The deal's not done till the money's in the bank' is a good rule of thumb for anyone in business. The skill is to get the money where it belongs in the way most attractive to the consumer.

RelTechnic 5: consumer retention/defection model

Once you have acquired a consumer the real hard work starts! This stage is really about turning the once-off consumer into a loyal consumer, and ideally a lifelong loyal consumer.

You need to plot every consumer's usage patterns: (1) why he/she uses the product; (2) how; (3) when; (4) where; and (5) how often. For instance, if it is a Mars chocolate bar, then the answers could be: (1) usually because I feel like one; (2) by eating it; (3) any time; (4) wherever I happen to be; and (5) as often as I feel like it (with 'mind your own business' added for good measure).

The answers are different if the purchase is a Berkeley Executive Home. They could be: (1) because all of the family agreed this was a lovely house in the right area; (2) by living there; (3) because we'd outgrown our old house; (4) I've just said, we like the area; and (5) we're here for life.

All the answers are made up, but you get the idea. What they indicate is the rich seam of information you can strike when you keep in close touch with consumers, close enough to be able to ask and get answers to those and other similar questions.

When you have completed your investigation into your consumers' usage patterns, the job of reworking out how to retain them becomes a practical proposition.

But what about consumers who have defected either by intent or indifference? You can then start to ask yourself the following questions:

1. 'Are we really doing sufficient to keep the loyalty of our consumers?'

   The obvious answers centre round price, product quality, product range, availability, packaging and point of sale, service where relevant, advertising and promotion strengths, competitive activity.

2. Let's say that those answers are all AOK. You should then ask yourself: 'Are we doing enough to make sure that our consumers are *aware* of all the good things they get from us and our products?'

   If the answer is no or only a tentative yes, you must remind yourself that pro-activity about consumer loyalty is essential. You should never assume that your products and service are so good they don't need publicity. Pro-activity about loyalty could lead you to consider whether you follow-up a purchase as often as you could. Follow-ups are essential when capital goods have been purchased – from a car to a computer. You should also consider whether you are making the most of cross-selling opportunities.

Consumer loyalty can often be retained, strengthened even, when products from other categories are offered and bought.

3. Another critical question: 'Do we make it easy for consumers with a problem to get a satisfactory answer?'

Ever tried raising a problem with a dotcom? Ever done the same with your local corner shop? Notice any difference? The response of the latter shows the way you that you should be going.

4. Do you make it easy for defected consumers to return?

BT, the UK's biggest telephone company, haemorrhaged consumers when the industry was opened up to all and sundry. BT fought back by making it completely easy for defectors to rejoin. All the prodigals had to do was ask, and they were welcomed back with open arms (only the fatted calf was missing). The TV advertising had a major contribution to make. It took care of any shyness about re-entry by emphasising that thousands were coming back to BT every day of the week. In other words, 'Join the trend, be part of the pack again'. It seems to be working, but the competition is getting fiercer.

Next question:

5. What did you do or not do that tempted your consumers to defect in the first place?

Competitive pressure? Or any of reasons suggested in 1. You can find some of the answers by contemplating your 'navel – it's amazing what a guilty conscience can bring to mind. But you should definitely augment introspection with research, preferably perhaps qualitative through consumer groups. When the answers come back, evaluate and act.

I mentioned cross selling as a way of retaining and perhaps strengthening loyalty. A company that satisfies demand across more than one product range may easily inspire extra loyalty. On the other hand, it could come a cropper. Virgin, past master at cross selling, has made little impact with its cola drink. W. H. Smith, the UK's biggest newsagent, failed to win loyalty with its ill-fated attempts to run a chain of superstores for do-it-yourself fans.

'All-to-One' via RelTechnics

The 'All-to-One' philosophy is the power behind each of those RelTechnics. It acts as a constant reminder that the aim of all the models and all the work you do in connection with them is to focus the strengths and attentions of the whole company and everyone in it on each individual consumer and do so in a way that entirely matches that consumer's lifestyle and requirements, now and into the future. It also reminds everyone involved with the application of RelTechnics that the marketing strategy/plan which evolves as a result must be fully integrated and methodically and consistently applied with the active support of everyone in the company, not just those facing the consumer directly.

In turn the results of using the techniques enable you and your company to achieve all those 'All-to-One' advantages – and to move up through the various RelModel levels. The information revealed by RelTechnics will give all your people a deeper, more practical understanding of consumers, how to create lifetime value for them and for you. It will show your people how their attitudes and assumptions should be shaped to match the realities of the market.

It should also convince them that consumer-orientation is the only future for any kind of business and that the consumer is final authority on everything. There is no superior court of appeal. The consumer's decision is final.

Case study

Sony found the gap

YOUR ON-GOING RESEARCH into your consumers' behaviour may unveil a gap where there are no consumers because there are no products, even though there is a potential need. You carefully define that need and design a product to fill it. Alternatively, you may simply have a bright idea which, subsequent research shows, fills a need no one was previously aware of. Or your research scientists, in blissful disregard for the basic rules of enlightened marketing, might come to you and say: 'Hey, we've invented this. Go out and sell it.' Scores of new markets have been created in one way or another in recent years. For example, until very recently, there was no market for digital cameras, or for scanners, or for mobile phones, or for hand-held computers – the products didn't exist. The markets were created partly as a result of technological breakthroughs, partly because the companies first involved had learnt from their research and their experience that such products could find consumers. Sometimes the innovating company promotes the new product category with such burning vigour as to create a *cordon sanitaire* of scorched earth round its newly created market. The classic 'keep-off' instance is the Sony Walkman, a great product with no competitors worth speaking of, just a rabble round the outside far from the centre where the real money is. No one can get near the Walkman consumer, either actual or prospective, so hot is the Sony Walkman name. Mr Sony, in addition to founding and running one of the world's great electronic enterprises, knew, understood, empathised with consumers wherever in the world they lived. This was an astonishing achievement for one man living on an island off the Asian mainland, someone whose knowledge of western culture could only be second hand, yet someone who had his finger on the pulse of teenagers and would-be teenagers everywhere including the west. Why? He'd done his research homework. In any case, the potential consumers out there, enormous numbers of them, were already his consumers for other electronic entertainment products. His new insight was

Case study (continued)

that young people liked to have music wherever they went and would pay for the wherewithal to have it. In short, he looked at the market from the potential consumer's point of view. He knew his company had the technology to deliver the ultra-lightweight tape player needed. The rest is history, profit for Sony and a major lesson for the rest of us – that we should always look at the market from the potential consumer's point of view.

Case study

L'Oréal

Getting closer to consumers in the Pacific Rim

HOW DO YOU penetrate new markets via the 'All-to-One' philosophy of getting closer to target consumers and retaining them?

L'Oréal, best known for its beauty products, has now transformed itself from a French-focused company to a global player. It has had particular success in the Pacific Rim where the policy of getting closer to the consumer, developing internal cultural weapons and keeping a metaphorical ear to the ground, has paid dividends.

In the early 1990s, L'Oréal identified the Asian Pacific region as a major new market. With economic growth and rapidly growing average incomes, the women of the region's burgeoning middle classes wanted more than just the basic soaps and toiletries, and they became more discerning about product quality and performance.

L'Oréal began to get closer to its potential markets in the region, closer to its consumers. It sought to understand them better and match its product portfolio more closely to consumer needs. What it found was pleasantly reassuring. Certainly, its corporate philosophy was to leverage its portfolio; it also knew that product performance and image had to match the culture and the consumer mindset of the market. But to its surprise, there was already an overall fit of brand portfolio to consumer requirements.

To project the performance and image of its products, L'Oréal used all relevant channels – main media advertising, point of sale and large-scale sampling. It made creative use of partners, working closely with retailers, hairdressers and opinion-formers such as journalists and VIPs, all treated as part of the insider group, members of the 'club' with privileged knowledge, and generally part of L'Oréal's own family providing feedback from the grass roots.

Even more significant was L'Oréal's realisation of the power of its own team and to inculcate in everyone the brand values and culture

Case study (continued)

of the Paris 'signature'. But with this proviso: the Paris personality with its sophisticated heritage of fashion, perfume and cosmetics had to merge all that with the intricacies and idiosyncrasies of each local market. Only then would there be a company culture that could maintain L'Oréal's traditional qualities and be accepted by all those who formed part of L'Oréal's extended family in the region ... only then could the local teams become brand champions. Recognition of the crucial role of these people and the consumers and prospects they in turn influenced enabled L'Oréal to strike the delicate balance between harmonising the brands internationally within the portfolio and energising the local entrepreneurial spirit to drive growth and share of the consumers' minds.

L'Oréal invests heavily in its people. It recruits locally, hiring the best talent with both business and people skills, and with more than a dash of creativity. Those selected are sent to Paris to absorb the L'Oréal culture first hand in its own home. Risk and possible failure are accepted as a part of this culture, and seen as inevitable accompaniments to innovative solutions and truly worthwhile new projects. And always, L'Oréal treats its people with the same enthusiasm and respect as it treats its brands.

The results are showing. L'Oréal is now a leading player in all its Asia Pacific markets.

I am grateful to Brand Warriors, *edited by Fiona Gilmore, for guidance on the above report.* Brand Warriors *is specially useful and interesting because it gives the story of each brand from the inside – the people telling the story were closely involved in the action described. In the case of L'Oréal, it was Alan Evrard, zone director for Africa and Asia Pacific.*

Six

Mastering the Internet with RelWeb

'The entire globe is now tied together in a single electronic market moving at the speed of light. There is no place to hide.'

Walter Wriston, former Citicorp Chairman

THE INTERNET, ALTHOUGH now appreciated as one medium among many, is still a powerful sales and marketing channel with a potential that is nowhere near realised. Forget the hype, this is the truth. Without mastery of this medium you are almost certainly on the way down and fast. That's now. As understanding of its true potential becomes more and more widespread and implemented, those without high Internet competency had better retire to the hills and breed goats. There'll be more money in the skins of pedigree Saanen billies and the healthy milk the nannies give than in trying to be in virtually any kind of business without an Internet capability.

This chapter recommends how best to acquire the capability you need. More precisely it describes how the Internet can be used as part of the total marketing mix to your best advantage and to fulfil all your 'All-to-One' aims, in particular the all-embracing aim of building lifelong, high-value consumer relationships.

The hero of the chapter is a model called RelWeb (yes, 'Rel' stands for relationship).

The RelWeb model

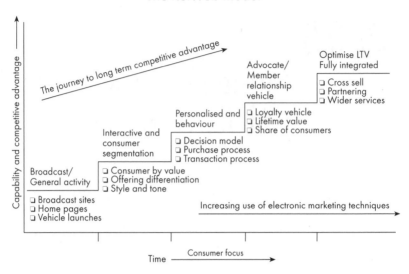

RelWeb is a model for Internet effectiveness. It deals with the five essential steps required to build those lifelong consumer relationships that are the culmination of the RelModel itself and should be the ultimate objective of every marketer. The five stages in the RelWeb correspond to the five stages of the RelModel and describe the development in the use of the Internet from the only just acceptable to perfection, or as near perfection as anyone is entitled to get. Like the RelModel, the RelWeb offers five points of entry. I urge you, as you read, to carry out the same self-examination (and company examination) that you did with RelModel. That examination will tell you where you are now in your use of the Internet and detail the way forward and upward.

Level 1: broadcast and tactical activity

At this level the website is providing mainly one-way information with little opportunity for consumer and information gathering. The

---

Worn out brochure-ware

All new media start by imitating old media. The Internet was no exception. At first it thought it was a shelf for brochures – at least that's how the majority of website designers saw it. People logging on saw brochures as a bore. Most sites are still boring!

---

site is product-centric, the corporate expression of what those within the company think of the company and its products, with the odd colour gizmo, flashes and snazzy graphics. Level 1 is the boasting level! The company is probably blinded by its IT department which has the by-now traditional technology mindset. The marketing team exists to provide the branding, brochures and product information – online. Effectively the site offers only 'brochure-ware', standard company information that can be obtained in other formats. There is also a strong element of brand image. The site contains basic consumer databases but with limited information. Typical information includes details of new products, special promotions and major company announcements (about acquisitions for instance), much of it merely brochure-ware, illustrating the company's not the consumer's view of the world.

Does any of the above sound familiar? If you can see yourself and your company lurking behind those words, you're in business, you've made a start. All you have to do now is move up to Level 2.

Level 2: consumer segmentation and interaction

As the website matures, the first interactive steps are taken. Prices and other detailed information are given – which encourages consumer interactivity. A start can be made on consumer segmentation and consumers can begin to 'see themselves' on the site, but as parts of a segment not as individuals with screens

Some more enlightened site designers stumbled over the fact that people were intelligent and began to respect them and cater for them. The consumer segmentation that characterises this level gives you a chance to make niche appeals with some interactivity. Niche people like to communicate with niche providers. It's a sort of club and the Internet is really good at providing club facilities.

dedicated to their interests. Consumers can be targeted by value, and the style and tone of the site can be adjusted accordingly. Consumer information can now be stored in a single central database. Interactive communication is now possible not only within the Internet but also between the Internet and other marketing channels. At this level, the Internet is used for developing brand and niche loyalty. It can be integrated into the information-gathering process as well as with other media and distribution channels.

If you're now at the stage described above, you're well on the way. Provided you're happy with your competency at Level 2, then you should chivvy your people up to Level 3 and make sure they fulfil all the requirements there.

Level 3: personalised and behaviour programmes

The website becomes more consumer-driven. Details of previous sales and transactions, now stored in the database, create a personal history for each consumer. This is used to generate new sales opportunities in a highly personalised format. The site now starts to demonstrate some e-commerce capabilities. At this level, the website is used to increase consumer loyalty and to understand consumer needs in terms of product development.

Loyalty must be worked at

> *Even the army doesn't take loyalty for granted! It has to be worked at. Your website should reward those who visit it. Make it easy for them. Tell them something they wouldn't otherwise know. Remind them that you are thinking of their needs now and into the future – and you can, because now you know so much about each consumer. But you can still ask them to tell you more.*

Level 3 is reasonably advanced, and far more advanced that most so-called e-expert companies can truly claim. When you feel that your company is at home there, it's time to move up to Level 4.

Level 4: advocate/member relationship

The benefits of the evolving consumer relationship start to increase. Specific benefits offered to consumers can be matched by their value (that is, the value of the consumer to the company), their motivations and their interests. The buying needs and purchasing cycles of individual consumers become better understood. The website can begin to offer loyalty clubs, user forums and such like with the intent of encouraging active input from consumers – who are becoming your advocates. Consumer input not only encourages empathy between that consumer and the site, and so further promotes loyalty, it also reassures would-be consumers that this is a good place to be and encourages them to become regular loyal visitors. Developments of this kind indicate that the lifetime value of each consumer is now more fully understood and evaluated.

Level 4 companies are making comparatively productive use of the Internet medium. With a little more effort, they could drop the 'comparatively' bit and move up to Level 5 where the full fruits of the Internet marketing experience await them.

Consumers are good at selling

Your best sales aid is a satisfied consumer. Online booksellers, Amazon, have taken this dictum to heart. More or less every book it sells has reviews from consumers. It works as well with anything. Take cars. Get people to give testimonials on screen – 'my first test drive'. It's worth many thousands of words of professionally written text.

Level 5: lifetime optimisation and cross selling

At this stage the lifelong value of the consumer relationship can be maximised. Loyalty can begin to be widened to include the consumer's partner and family through targeted communications, marketing and sales activities. The expanding consumer database means a wider choice of products and services can be made available. Consumers now expect a highly personalised service based around their stated preferences. They feel at home at the site – they 'own' it and are happy to contribute ideas, make complaints and show how things could be improved. E-commerce forms a more important element in selling and marketing activity. A site operating at this level can be used to create additional revenue, maximise profitability, plan future offerings and defend market position.

Your RelWeb ranking

Evaluating where you are against each level of RelWeb capability is important, but what could be even more crucial is how your ranking compares with that of your competitors. Comparisons on web functionality, versatility and interactivity – you versus your competitors – are possible at relatively low cost. Comparisons of the full marketing mix of all media, all service interaction and so forth

Consumers as partners

> *Websites are ideal for involving your consumers in your company. Each of them can tell you what they like about you, what they don't, and what you could do to improve things all round. Consumers have no vested interest except their own. And people are usually honest when they talk about their vested interest. You've a lot to learn from them and the Internet is the place to do the learning.*

would be hugely time-consuming, difficult to produce accurately and regularly, and would be very expensive. That's another way the Internet scores.

Website comparisons on the other hand are comparatively scientific. They can be carried out on short time-scales and are easily repeatable at regular intervals. The EDS Consumer Focus Group has created and is now implementing just such a system of website comparison – RelDex. RelDex, initially created for the automobile industry, is in fact a very versatile tool for indexing the relative capability of any kind of enterprise to develop relationship functionality on their websites.

How to section your website

There are so many good how-to-create-your-website books on the market. I'm not going to repeat what they have to say. They'll tell you quickly enough and it's beyond the remit I gave myself in writing this book.

The cuckoo in the media nest

C ULTS ARE LIKE cuckoos. They can't abide competition. The minute the cuckoo is big enough, it turns on its fellow fledglings and turfs them out. There's only room for one bird in the nest, and that's the cuckoo.

In the media world as in the natural world, this in-comes-the-cuckoo-out-go-the-others cycle constantly repeats itself. Take television. That was the Internet of the 1950s, the cult to end all cults, the medium to outperform all others, whether for news, entertainment, culture (all brows), games, companionship, advertising, you name it, television was best. Radio? No one ever listens. Print? Old hat! Newspapers and magazines couldn't compete and many were putting up the shutters. Direct mail was junk. Fax was a spelling mistake. Literature was something your less-clever friends read at university. Cinema was dying (why pay to see a bad film at the cinema when you can stay at home and see a bad film for nothing?). Telephones were what old ladies used. Sales people were redundant (the growth of the supermarket proved it: you entered the store primed by the TV advertising and took off the shelf the products you'd seen on the screen – the only function of what used to be called sales assistants was to take your money and, with luck, help you to the car with the trolley).

Advertising agency presentations to clients always began with the TV schedule (which invariably took the lion's share of the appropriation – and then some). The main course, the *pièces de résistance*, were the proposed TV commercials. On came the top creative brass doing their stuff in spades. When the client was sufficiently befuddled by the brilliance of the agency's use of the premier selling medium, the juniors were wheeled in, rather shamefacedly, to expose the print ads and things called 'leaflets', a typically dismissive term for anything non-TV, and perhaps the radio commercials. Remember: virtually the only radio stations in those days that took advertising were aimed largely at teenagers. Clients weren't teenagers so were more bemused than usual by what they were asked to approve. Conversation was about the TV. Nothing else really mattered.

Those interested in ancient history (the rest of you can skip this bit) may like to hear about the late, great Lord Thomson, First Baron Thomson of Fleet as his friends didn't call him, but, known around Toronto where he ran radio stations and newspapers as Our Roy, son of a local barber who had immigrated from the UK. When Roy re-immigrated, he bought some more newspapers including *The Scotsman* and later *The Times*. In 1957 the government awarded him the contract to transmit commercial television throughout Scotland. He said later, and wished he hadn't, that owning a commercial TV station was like owning a licence to print money. TV had become by then the glamour medium bar none. Roy clearly had nothing against TV. It was making him a mountain of money. But he saw that its dominance was bad for business in the long term and, probably in the short term as well, for his newspapers. Part of the problem, as he correctly realised, was the belief that TV represented the future and other media the past. Roy's answer was to launch colour supplements for his Sunday newspaper – TV was still black and white – and per-suade the marketers through their weakest point, the softest touch, the creative people in the advertising agencies. 'Get those trendies on the side of press ads and the job's done', figured Roy. He figured well. TV, fortified shortly by its own colour, went from strength to strength, but so did press advertising. Good sense had prevailed, and the marketers also against their will, regained more choice.

That was television that was. Now watch history repeat itself.

Come the 1980s and the in-thing is database marketing, made possible by ever-increasing and ever-cheapening computer power. The smart money poured in, the bandwagon almost broke its axles under the weight, evangelists proclaimed the end of brands, and the marketing trendies began to practise saying 'one-to-one', though some also said, 'Hang on, we've got the technology, why don't we set up vast telephone centres and get interactive with the consumer – then we really will be talking one-to-one.'

And so it came to pass. Call centres were top of the 'future-has-arrived' pile for a time, and long may they stay near the top – until technology came up with its latest wonder, the Internet, which, of course, as its devotees claim, kicks everything else into touch.

Will we never learn?

The world is vast. Billions of individuals live in it. They're the potential market. But every one of those individuals has a near infinity of moods, attitudes, needs, interests, hopes, ambitions, desires – consult *Roget's Thesaurus* for all other possible attributes of human beings. However, they have only a finite amount of time – 24 hours will remain the daily ration for the foreseeable future. As marketers, we have a vast and growing array of ways to communicate and persuade that near infinite number of prospects in that finite amount of time. We need all those ways, the more the better, why restrict ourselves? The fact is, we have no choice. Human beings will not be corralled into a pen labelled 'Internet user' any more than they agreed to stay in pens labelled 'TV watcher' or 'Telephone addict'. One medium, one approach, one way of communication soon palls. Sometimes, people like being interrupted. Variety is the spice of their life and so it must be of marketing communications because variety is what individuals demand and what products and services need if they are to be effectively marketed.

Which reminds me – creativity! Selling anything is not simply a matter of conveying information, which the Internet is good at, or even 'mood and tone', at which the Internet is not so good, at least not yet. It is, additionally and critically, a matter of how that information or that mood and tone are conveyed. In a word, it is about creativity.

Now, the superb thing about the Internet from where the marketer stands is that the prospect *chooses* to access it. There's no compulsion about it, no necessity, nothing subliminal. It's courteous, non-interruptive, open and above board. Prospects in effect have given you permission to communicate with them. Can there be a better opening for a sales pitch (the right kind of sales pitch, of course). It's a great example of permission marketing, about which Seth Godwin has written his fascinating book (it's reviewed on page 260). As Seth reminds us: 'Every marketing campaign gets better when an element of permission is added.' The Internet scores very high on this 'permission to communicate' scale.

It scores much worse on the creativity scale. I'm talking about things as they are, not as they might be or will be. I'll come to the future later. At present, marketing communications on the Internet pale besides those in other media. At any particular site, the visitor gets information by the bucketful. Of warmth, heart, empathy, humour, beauty, style, charm, character, all the qualities that can make advertising work so well in other media, there is little evidence, or at least, much less than there should be. The information given on a company's website is nearly always good, full and reliable. The advertising on the same website, on any website, is at the creative level achieved by the sandwich-board man. Banner advertisements on the Internet are a bit like the things you see towed by low-flying aircraft over a crowded beach at the seaside.

Of course, it will change. Some genius will show us how Internet advertising can equal any other in its power, impact, charm, wit, persuasiveness, *creativity*. But that genius hasn't appeared yet. And we have to work in the world as we find it. In any case, by the time the Internet has matured and offers us the creative possibilities now taken for granted in most other media, some other form of technical wizardry will have broken through, something no one today has even fantasised about, something that will transform people's lives and outdate everything else and certainly push the Internet off its perch – WAP, TV, embedded technology, thought-wave transference technology – your guess is as good as the next guy's.

Let's wait until it happens. Meantime, the media that television 'killed off' in the last century are stronger than ever in this. There are more newspapers and magazines than ever before (thanks to the new technologies, of course) and far more are sold. And read. And kept hanging around the house for everyone to glance at or pick up or cut things out of. There are more cinemas, more radio stations, more outdoor advertising sites, more direct mail, more emphasis on sales professionals, more everything that can help a provider of something to communicate with a possible user of that something. And there is, of course, more need than ever for the providers to make sure their communication with the potential user rises above all the competitive noise, and is understood, then acted on. Where you put your message is vitally important. *How* you communicate your message in whatever medium you choose is a matter of life or death for the company.

Seven

Media and the RelModel

HOW DO YOU choose your media? You must answer three questions.

1. Which medium has the qualities that are appropriate for your consumer group, your message and the way you want to deliver it?

2. Which format is most suitable?

3. Which of the suitable formats offer the most cost-effective help at the different levels of the RelModel?

So, to get us started, here is my list of qualities (to help you answer the first question) that may be held by different media. You may have your own list, but I doubt whether it will differ in too much detail from this:

Absorbing

Borrowed

Casual

Demanding

Flexible

General

High quality

Addictive

Bought

Cost-effective

Entertaining

Free

Group

Hired

Inexpensive	Informative
Instructive	Interactive
International	Keepable
Likeable	Local
Mass market	Metropolitan
Movie	Multimedia
Owned	Portable
Print	Regular
Relaxing	Self-selective
Solitary	Sound only
Specialist	State of the art
Still	Tactile
Target specific	Throwaway
Traditional	Transactional
User friendly	

Those are the qualities capable of being possessed by different media formats.

Now for the formats (the second question) themselves:

Books	Cards in shops, etc.
Catalogues	Clubs/associations
Cinema	Conferences
Daily (paid for) newspapers	Direct mail
Directories	Events (including charity events)
Exhibitions	Freebies
Interactive TV	Internet (Intranet/Extranet)
Kiosks	Literature
Magazines	Mcomms
Packaging	Point of sale
Presentations	Product placement
Promotional items	Public relations
Radio	Retail outlets
Roadside posters	Sales and service representatives

Signage	Sports sponsorship
Staff uniforms	Stationery
Sunday newspapers	Supermarket floors
Telephones including WAPs/mobiles	
Teletext	Tickets (till, entrance, travel, etc.)
TV	Vehicle livery
Video/DVD	Wall charts
Word of mouth	

You are now able to create your own simple SWOT chart of the strengths, weaknesses, opportunities and threats for each of the media available to you, making your assessment in the light of your target consumer profiles. Your SWOT chart will give a quick qualitative overview of the media appropriate for your needs. It should be used in conjunction with a hard-nosed quantitative assessment, that is an assessment based on the hard objective facts – absolute cost, cost per thousand, reach, coverage, timing, context.

The RelModel as a whole divides media into its own categories, five of them, as follows:

❑ Level 1 – offer undifferentiated mass communication.

❑ Level 2 – offer opportunities for segmented communications that are more relevant and better timed.

❑ Level 3 – relate more closely to the target's lifestyle.

❑ Level 4 – allow interactive relationships.

❑ Level 5 – allow complete 'All-to-One' symbiotic interaction for cross selling.

It's obvious that the categories overlap somewhat and that most media come under more than one category – which is why media selection is as much an art form as it is a science. It is also obvious that the way the message is presented can either work with or against the grain of the media used. To give an extreme example: an advertisement for an antiseptic in a popular newspaper would not contain full details of the clinical trials that indicated its effectiveness; an advertisement for the same product in a medical magazine would not consist of a simple slogan and a photograph of a relaxed mum.

But the essential point is that the RelModel uses these categories cumulatively. Level 1 uses Level 1 media only, but Level 2 uses both Level 1 and Level 2 media, until at Level 5 all media comes within the remit. At Level 5 it is 'All-to-One' with a vengeance. The mistake of the 1:1 crusaders and their Internet followers is to put 1:1 interactive communication as the only ideal. The 'All-to-One' ideal is to use the combination chosen from all available media that will best meet your marketing needs.

So, as I go through each of the media, I'll give each one an Egon Ronay-type mark to show on which of the RelModel levels they work best. I'd better add here that there are any number of first-rate textbooks on media. This chapter is not meant to offer them any competition. I am simply trying to show how the RelModel can help you in your choice of media.

Books   *RelModel Levels 4–5*

Books, the kind you see in bookshops and keep on meaning to buy, don't usually feature on advertising schedules, but that, very occasionally, could be a mistake. Certainly there are no quick results to be gained from a book about your product or service, but in the right circumstances with the right product the long-term effect could be very worthwhile. The formidable no-holds-barred Joseph Kennedy told his son to write a book to prove to the East Coast intellectuals (he used a ruder phrase) that he was a serious contender for the Presidency.

Books are now par for the course in the publicity build-up for any would-be American President, in fact for anyone running for high office in the developed world. Books about cars and car manufacturers have their value in building the prestige of the marque or in providing background. Cookery books featuring your products are obviously useful especially if you happen to be Sainsbury's. Books about esoterically interesting hobbies such as falconry, archery or mediaeval manuscripts, if your products or services impinge on such areas, stand a fair chance of being bought by the aficionados.

However, the short answer to 'the book or no book' question includes the words 'money' and 'time'. There's a drama inherent in every product or service and this drama is capable of being turned into a book by the right author. There have been good books written about cornflakes, soap products, oil and petrol, but they were about the generic not the branded versions. Probably only an already established organisation – a grand hotel, a famous chain of estate agents, a newspaper or a major industrial concern, one with money and time to spare – could really benefit from a reasonably sized (say 200 pages) hardback. People might just be tempted to buy/borrow and read such a book because it's about something they already know a little about. And it's an odd fact of human nature that people usually like to learn more about something about which they already know a little rather than plunge into the totally unknown.

But a book about a new cough medicine, or a new chain of newsagents? Perhaps not, unless there were something revolutionary about the medicine or the newsagents (an intriguing thought).

On the other hand, if you have an interestingly different product or service, one that needs some explanation, you could commission a smallish paperback and offer it in a promotion as a give-away. But there are probably better ways of spending your time and money.

The major exceptions to all this are the manuals which usually arrive with the product, but can be bought separately in an expanded form. Individual makes of car have real books written about them, usually by enthusiasts and usually when the car has achieved some sort of historic renown. Another kind of exception is provided courtesy of Sir Richard Branson. Books about him and his exploits make important contributions to the commercial success of his companies. But there aren't too many Richard Bransons about.

Cards in shops, post offices, etc.   *RelModel Levels 3–5*

For letting your flat to a bunch of students or airport workers without paying an agent, or finding your lost cat, or getting an old boy to do a few hours keeping your garden up to scratch or telling people about the bring-and-buy sale at the local scout hut, there is nothing like a card. It is exactly the best medium. It is targeted locally, it has a reference (i.e. you know precisely who's behind it because there's the name), it has local relevance and offers quick returns. What's more, people actually walk over to read them – another example of permissive marketing. They have asked to be told and perhaps even sold.

Catalogues   *RelModel Levels 1–5*

Imagine living in America's Wild West at the start of the last century, isolated on your ranch, tens of miles from the nearest neighbour and hundreds from a city. Into that wilderness came the catalogue, landing with a colossal thump on your porch. It brought the city store right there into your life, into your very living room. Whatever you wanted you could buy and have delivered without having to leave home. Sounds familiar? Yes sir, the Sears, Roebuck catalogue (the outstanding name) was what Internet shopping is today, the home-lovers answer to getting the jalopy out and braving the coyotes and dust-storms (then) and the traffic jams and traffic wardens (now). Reprints of those early catalogues are now prized coffee-table exhibits. In fact catalogues still are. Catalogue enthusiasts have made and continue to make the mail-order companies of today very successful indeed, thank you. It's hard for the non-enthusiast to see why, but it's something to do with the size and sheer 'heft' of the catalogue itself (the tactility as the psychologists say). It breathes prosperity, almost as if you own all the products simply by owning their idealised photographs in their idealised settings in that luxuriously physical, touchable, smellable catalogue – eat your heart out, Internet. Then there's the extra pleasure of leafing through the pages with a friend or relative, and leaving the page open showing the chosen desired product for your partner just to happen to see.

Catalogues work in virtually every product category. The biggest is probably clothes, followed by household products, toys of course, hobby items, specialist areas like wedding clothes, then baby wear and equipment, toys, fishing gear, books, the list is really endless. They sell huge amounts of product, sufficiently huge to justify the comparatively high print costs – though they are minimal compared with the cost of the sales staff and real estate they replace.

Catalogue marketing can be stand-alone – as discussed above – or adjunct to a normal business, say a high-street retail chain. The stand-alone variety is a very specialised business with some extremely powerful operators very firmly in place. Beginners keep out.

Catalogues as an adjunct are a less formidable challenge, but their benefits both to supplier and consumer are similar to those of the stand-alone. You can target the recipients very precisely using good databases. The catalogues themselves allow browsing, encourage word of mouth, have a fairly long life – up to a year – and you can either offer home delivery or encourage prospects into your stores. You can experiment with pricing and with regional variations of both pricing and product.

You can also introduce a club element, either by offering discounts to people who band together to buy products from the catalogue over a period or by appointing 'leaders' in a particular area who collate orders from friends, relatives and neighbours and themselves receive special discounts or other rewards.

Smaller tactical or niche catalogues can provide a very flexible addition to your marketing armoury. Catalogues can easily be added to a campaign – say connected to a large sporting event where you can special-edition apparel with your banding or logo. Get the imagination going. Synergy between the catalogue and your other programmes could reap dividends.

Clubs/associations   *RelModel Levels 4–5*

The instinct to join a group of people with similar tastes, interests, problems, aspirations, whatever, is very human, very basic and very powerful. But be warned. Almost as powerful is the basic human instinct to drop out of the group when the benefits of membership are not forthcoming, or when some other group appears to offer more of the same but better, cheaper and more convenient. So there are two challenges, to get the club up and running, and then to keep it running.

You can set up your own club or association and link it directly with your business – book clubs are the obvious example, but there are many others, including wine clubs, holidays (time share for instance) and records, of course. Manufacturers of certain kinds of 'enthusiast' products, such as sports cars, motorboats, fishing gear, can form or encourage associations whose aim is to help people get more fun and value out of the products. You may need to call in specialist advice in the setting up and probably in the running too.

As an alternative, or in addition, you can piggyback in some way or other with an existing club or association. Their number is legion, ranging from Rotary to the Women's Institute, from the Automobile Association to the local golf club. The initial task is to persuade the officials of the club or association that your company is one whose name they want to link with theirs. From then on, you have a clear field. You can work to determine the most productive depth of involvement – from taking advertisements in their newsletter or magazine to organising special offers and discounts. With local groups especially, you may also be expected to make ex gratia payments to their funds. And why not? Your mission statement undoubtedly contains a reference to being a good citizen – here's another opportunity to show you mean it.

That is a more important point than it may seem. In today's complaining and litigious society, companies need to keep their 'licence to operate' in good order. Support for and approval by an independent organisation with a clear social purpose and sound local or national reputation is good public relations anyway and it certainly helps justify the licence.

A good club/association tie-up can bring you many benefits. You have a willing audience for whatever messages you care to send or offers you care to make. What's more you already have that audience taped. You know their demographics and psychographics. You know them more or less by name. You know what they bought last time. It's all joy, or at least as much joy as you are likely to get when dealing with fickle human beings.

Cinema   *RelModel Levels 1–5*

The cinema is the young person's medium par excellence (if by young you mean someone under 35) and is usually the most cost-effective way of reaching that age group. Attendances are good and cover all the socio-economic classes. It is also – at the time of writing as these things change rapidly – a prestige, fashionable medium, something to be talked about at work next day. But even all that is only half the story.

A cinema is the diametric opposite of a one-to-one medium – it is one-to-hundreds. Go to the cinema and you're one of the crowd and pleased to be in it. The cinema audience is already hyped up by the prospect of the film it is going to watch. Moreover, it is hyped up as a totality. There is a kind of mass enthusiasm, better described as a mass responsiveness which can make or break your advertising. One rude noise in the middle of your oh-so-sensitive commercial can sink it. One belly laugh at your funny commercial and you're made. Whatever, the commercials had better be good. They will be compared with the forthcoming films, and films have rarely been better scripted, cast, designed and made than they are now.

Product placement in the films is a good and current genre to support your main campaign – I even saw a competition and prize draw leaflet accompanying a product placement campaign linked to Ben Elton's 'Maybe Baby' – highly integrated and impactful.

However, the more immediate competition comes from the other commercials surrounding yours. Unlike TV, which sprinkles the commercials throughout its programmes in groups of four or five (at least they do in the UK), cinemas bundle all that night's commercials into one marathon session before the main fare of the evening is presented.

Cinema should not be done in isolation, because it doesn't give you enough repetition. It needs reinforcement – from TV and print advertising.

Conferences   *RelModel Levels 4–5*

Conferences are good because, like exhibitions, they tend to attract the committed, the interested and the influential. They are better than exhibitions in some ways – you can target your invitations and they are very interactive.

Organising conferences is a highly skilled job – don't attempt it unless you're prepared to fail. Better by far to get a professional company in. The golden rules remain the same. They are:

1. Impeccable arrangements, with everything happening on time, refreshments as promised, equipment tested and in full working order.

2. One overall, overriding message to emerge whatever arabesques individual speakers might care to make – and don't allow the conference to be a shop window for the speakers. It's your company's show.

3. Vet all the speeches beforehand to ensure that rule 2, above, is followed.

4. If possible, have a well-known MC and the most famous, best-regarded guru as lead speaker.

5. Give delegates a chance to make their presence felt either in the main sessions or in working groups.

6. Deliver a printed report of proceedings to all who attend with extra copies for their boss.

7. And always, always follow up, either by post, e-mail or phone.

Daily (paid for) newspapers   *RelModel Levels 1–5*

The best advertisement gives news about a product or service. Where better to place it than in a daily newspaper whose prime function is to give news (Sunday newspapers are less about news more about a good read). Newspaper readers expect to be given new information. They are in the mood to read what you have to say. The fact that your advertisement appears next to news about the outside world makes it appear relevant, contemporary and all those other good things. This is why the dotcoms spend so much money advertising their wares in newspapers – when they are not spending even more money advertising them on television.

Readers trust the newspaper they buy and read every day. It really is a kind of friend and companion. For many, it provides company on the journey to work. To others it's a familiar visitor into the home. Something of that relationship of trust and friendship spreads over your advertisement. Subconsciously, and sometimes consciously, the reader thinks, 'well if the newspaper is prepared to print the advert, it must be OK'.

Newspapers cannot give you the scope of specialisation provided by magazines. Racing fans and business people have their own specialist daily paper. For the rest, the only specialisation is geographical, with most national newspapers having regional editions and most regions having their own daily and/or evening newspaper.

Research into newspaper readership is regularly updated and very thorough, so thorough that the unsuspecting can be led into false economies. For instance, research may tell you that you can reach more beekeepers at less cost per head through a national newspaper than through a magazine that specialises in bee keeping. The bean counters say go for the national newspaper. The discerning know that even a beekeeper is in no mood to go apiarist in a crowded underground train. Sit him or her in garden shed with a glass of something pleasant and a copy of the 'Bee-Keeper', or whatever, and you have a potential consumer. This may be an obvious example, but media selection remains an art as well as a science.

Newspapers used to suffer from poor printing and lack of colour. Both those handicaps have gone, although the paper quality does not equal that of a good magazine, which will always have the edge on good colour photograph reproduction.

There's a general point to be made about all traditional media, one which the Internet enthusiasts are quite justified in making. The success of traditional media in reaching their target markets and as a result in attracting advertising sometimes results in 'too many advertisements' in any one issue or round any one programme or at any one outdoor site. The media owners have an interest in restricting the amount of advertising. After all, people do not usually buy their newspapers, etc. or watch their programmes just to get exposed to advertising. But just occasionally their need for advertising revenue perhaps outplays their need to keep the right editorial/advertising balance in their titles. On the other hand (you need two hands in this business), particularly in the case of magazines, the advertisements are as intrinsically interesting and attractive as much of the editorial. Vogue would be a less good read without the advertisements.

The ultimate answer is that an individual will pay attention to an advertisement if it is seen to offer something worthwhile. The ultimate task of the advertiser is to make sure that the advertisements do just that.

Direct mail   *RelModel Levels 2–5*

The most maligned medium of all. That's because it's intrusive, it has the nerve to come into your space without invitation – so it needs to be courteous, above all it needs to make a worthwhile promise and make it quickly. If it does that, it can be very effective, very targeted, very measurable. Intrusiveness is a double-edged sword and needs to be treated with care. The recipients know exactly what they getting. The sender, thanks to the precision and comprehensiveness of mailing lists, can judge very accurately who is receiving it. Assessment of overall cost-effectiveness is comparatively easy, certainly much easier than with most media.

Intellectuals may sneer, but people generally like getting 'personalised commercial' mail. It would be surprising if they didn't. After all, a good mail shot is specifically designed to interest a carefully targeted individual. The anti-direct-mail attack is sometimes narrowed to those with competitions. But people aren't stupid. They know very well that their chance of winning one of the fabulous prizes offered is pretty minimal, but so what? With very little effort, they can have their name put into the hat, and gain some frisson of excitement and all for no cost. Lonely people look out for the direct mail to arrive, No one else writes to them. But in fact very few people, lonely or otherwise, are displeased to get a letter or parcel with their name on it (provided the spelling's correct). Direct mail starts off well.

How well it continues, how long the gap between it being opened and binned depends on the subject matter and the promotional 'idea', the creativity. To get the right kind of creativity you need to employ the right kind of creative people, but how to do that is beyond the scope of this book. You'll know them when they've produced their first ideas.

Some products, often those with a 'serious' edge, lend themselves to direct mail. They include those concerned with finance of one kind or another, health, charities, books, all of them topics on which the chosen recipient is likely to be prepared to devote some time. On the principle that 'orthodoxy is my doxy and heterodoxy is yours', I divide the direct mail I receive into 'junk mail' – mail that doesn't interest me and 'non-junk mail' – mail that does. The science of successful direct mail, of course, is to send it only to those you know are interested in the subject being covered and to send it at the most relevant time, but mistakes do happen. The art of successful direct mail is to create material that speaks as from one interested person to another. A piece of direct mail really is a one-to-one communication, though it can't be tailored to suit individual needs in the same way as an Internet communication.

Direct mail is measurable, accountable and can be used to transfer the value of a mass awareness or positioning campaign achieved with TV or PR into targeted personal communications capable of converting a prospect into one of your consumers.

Direct mail can be costed very precisely, but the costs can be high. They can be mitigated by piggybacking (great word) with another company's shots. A favourite combination is to 'stuff' the direct mail shot into the bills sent out regularly by, for instance, the utilities.

The contrast is in your favour. Whatever you have to talk about, it must be more pleasing than the figures on the bills preceded by a pound sign.

Brilliant direct mail will explode your bottom line. Bad or misguided direct mail will cost heavily and ruin any credibility your brand has.

Directories   *RelModel Levels 4–5*

Directories, whether telephone, business or geographical, are good reference media especially for products/services catering for distress needs ('Quick, get a plumber, the bath's overflowing and I can't turn the tap off'). They are usually supplied free, but because people choose to consult them, in fact they usually need to consult them, and in a hurry too, you have their implied permission to plug your wares. They have a long life, a year or more, and become almost a permanent feature around the house. If you are aiming at the distress market, then the basic requirements of your advertisement are not so much size or colour (though both help) but quick recognition and instant understanding – there's no time for subtlety when the water is pouring out of the bathroom. However, directories are valuable advertising media even if you are not in the distress business. Entertainment, shopping, sports, games, hobbies, all the everyday needs of living can get people consulting a directory of one kind or another. Advertising space is usually inexpensive.

Events (including charity events)   *RelModel Levels 4–5*

An event can be anything from a drinks party for a few consumers in a handy restaurant to a banquet at the Mansion House, from a sponsored tennis tournament on the local courts to Wimbledon, from a local celebrity opening a new branch of your sportswear chain to the Queen opening a new art gallery (which your company has helped to sponsor). You can organise your own, or plug into someone else's. It can be directly linked to your business (like a wine tasting at a new wine bar), or not (like a box at Ascot for successful car distributors).

Organising your own is a major undertaking, though there are plenty of companies who will do it for you, for a fee. The benefits are obvious: you can invite anyone you like; tailor the action to suit your needs; cover the location with your publicity; claim all the credit in the resulting PR. The downside is the cost and the risks always attendant when a company strays outside its own expertise.

Plugging into an established event is a much more quantifiable venture. You know the type and size of the attendance. You can profit from previous years' experience, either your own or other people's. Your contribution, apart from money, will be your own publicity – which, as at Grand Prix meetings, need often be no more than having your posters displayed round the track. It's a safer bet all round.

On the other hand, if you do get an event going year after year, the returns can be enormous. I don't suppose Stella Artois minds spending money on its pre-Wimbledon tournament.

We could, I suppose, include 'stunts' under events. Those who are less than enthusiastic about Richard Branson's success might call his attempts to capture this record or that – in balloons or powerboats – as stunts. But the publicity gained is worth billions.

Exhibitions   *RelModel Levels 1–5*

A stand at an exhibition is a major commitment and can be a complete waste of money. The space is expensive. Design and building it burn money. You commit staff to service the stand for days on end, and produce reams of literature for them to hand out to visitors who then throw it away. And you've still to account for the entertaining.

So don't fall for the exhibition organiser's sales talk unless you are reasonably sure that the returns justify the investment. The points to consider are: Does the exhibition itself have sufficient prestige in your market sector and generally? Will your stand attract the clients and prospects you wouldn't otherwise get to meet? Will competitors cash in on your absence? Do you have new products to display? Can you win worthwhile media coverage from the stand?

If your answers are generally positive, good, because your company's presence at an exhibition can be very productive – provided your stand is imaginative, and provided you follow up every lead generated. You could get plenty. You meet people when they're in a frame of mind that's both relaxed and focused – no telephone calls or urgent meetings to distract. You can show off your full range of products and services, including anything new and especially anything complex. Where applicable, you can give demonstrations. You can hand out literature, but do it with some restraint – the collect-anything brigade are out in force at all exhibitions. And with your competitors all around, you can see where you are ahead, and where you're lagging.

Freebies   *RelModel Levels 1–5*

Free newspapers, delivered to the door or picked up at, say, railway stations have all the characteristics of paid-for newspapers but in a very minor key. Media that people get by chance and for nothing command less respect than media that people deliberately choose and hand over good money for. Advertising in freebies does have one virtue. It doesn't cost much.

Interactive TV   *RelModel Levels 4–5*

Interactive TV, in effect the conversion of the TV screen into a computer screen with access to the Internet, has been a dream for years and will shortly become an important reality. I can see the limitations. It's bad enough now getting the family to agree which programme to watch. When one member wants to get interactive, it will be worse. The solution must be to have more TV screens per house. So far as the marketers are concerned, interactive TV is just another way of delivering the Internet. Its prime importance will be in making even more people feel at home with it. There's another bonus: with the help of something like an immediately interactive quiz show, you can check whether your prospect is still with you.

This medium is just starting off and it is going to be exciting to see where it will go – definitely watch this space and take it very seriously.

Internet   *RelModel Levels 4–5*

Notice that I'm putting Internet in its place as yet another possible marketing medium, no more, no less. If we are to get the most out of it as a marketing medium, we have to show how it can work with other media synergistically (and it certainly can). We want no cuckoos in our media nest. You can use this at Levels 1, 2 or 3 but you really need to get your use of it at Levels 4 and 5. Any earlier and the capability of your organisation to make full use of its interactivity is really misplaced – you are better off sticking to combinations of media that match the capability of the organisation. Brochure-ware as at Level 1 does you no favours.

OK, so the Internet is just another medium. But what a medium! It's only been around a matter of months, yet already there are billions of people online worldwide and using its facilities for hours every day, though for over all those billions the average is under one hour. When TV got going again after the Second World War, the pundits marvelled at the phenomenal growth in the number of set-owners. It was nothing compared to growth in the number of computer owners and the numbers of people online to the Internet.

I'll deal with the drawbacks first. The first and most obvious is that technology is still less than 100 per cent efficient. Just read the book by Tim Berners-Lee (the hailed inventor of the Internet) to see the inadequacies that frustrate him. The hardware and the software at home can go down. So can the equipment at the Internet Service

Provider (ISP). And the network is far from infallible. But these are teething troubles. Soon – and neither Tim nor I know when – the Internet will be as reliable and taken for granted as TV is today.

Then there's the drawback that you can't determine accurately the market you are addressing. The reason is that it's the market, or rather the online individuals, who decide whether they want to be addressed. Your creativity has to work harder as a result, because it's the way you design your site and its contents that decides who accesses it. Or at least partly decide it. What also counts is the way you use other media to persuade people onto your site. This whole arena has become very, very competitive – even cluttered.

So far as determining the market you are addressing, the traditional media don't score much better on the research front than does the Internet, and much of the demographic and psychographic data they provide have to be taken with discretion. The fact for instance that X million ABC males buy a particular magazine and X times Y read it, is no guarantee that all those people actually read your advertisement.

The Internet, of course, has to cope with technophobia, especially among the older of us (those over 25). Children from three years upwards have no fear about computers and the Internet. They pick up the requisite skills at nursery school. Their parents find the skills harder to acquire. Some will never succeed. Most will. 'Computer literacy' is at the top of every educationalist's hit list. The skill problem will gradually disappear. The telephone had similar problems, and they have disappeared, more or less.

But even when the skill is there, accessing the Internet requires effort. Other media are effort-free, or very nearly so. Watching TV makes few demands, reading maybe a few more. Radio you can enjoy when you're doing something else. But the Internet requires concentration and alertness. Five years from now, when the novelty has gone, the Internet may be thought something of a drag, even when it's accessed from the sofa via the TV screen. You'll still have to keep on fiddling with the buttons, you still have to work at it. But now, that concentration and alertness act in our favour. Internet onliners are wide-awake to whatever you have to offer, and because it is they who seek you out, not the other way round, you have their permission to speak. Above all, you can talk to and be with your individual consumers and prospects in that well-publicised one-to-one environment, which as I've revealed elsewhere often has many drawbacks of its own. But, treated properly as a component in a bigger all-round marketing effort, it's a great advantage.

There are other advantages. You can learn a lot about your consumers and prospects. You can update material as good as instantly. And you can tailor your offer to individual consumers (the one-to-one effect).

The Internet is superb at business-to-business communication. Many of the world's largest corporations and hundreds of thousands of smaller ones already use it to invite – and accept – tenders for equipment. No other medium can give instant access to literally every supplier who wants to be there. No other medium allows inventory lists to be updated by the minute and available worldwide. No other medium allows these important deals to be carried out so quickly, efficiently and in complete privacy. The Internet would justify its existence simply as a B2B communication tool.

But the final word about the Internet is that there is no final word. The medium has just begun. Come back in five years' time. You might see a different beast. In the meantime, make the most of what it's got now. It's a lot.

This whole book is about winning in the post-Internet economy – the economy where the Internet is taken for granted. The winners will be those who make the most of the Internet within an overall media mix.

Internet types

Intranet and Extranet are types of Internet, the former only accessible within the enterprise, the latter accessible within the enterprise and among selected outsiders, such as key consumers, Both types can be used to carry information and dialogue too sensitive for general consumption. And because people like being privy to privileged information, the fact that both types are 'restricted' gives them significant power.

Kiosks   *RelModel Levels 2–5*

Kiosks at airports, shopping malls, bus stations, exhibitions and conferences and in fact anywhere that people gather to wait, work, talk or shop are an increasingly important communication medium, with several unique advantages. A kiosk is a simple construct – usually somewhat bigger than its telephone counterpart, stationed prominently and strategically in a place where people might be inclined to stop, look and enter. The simplest kiosks show advertisements and offer goodies such as free samples, competition entry and, of course, literature, plus perhaps a sales pitch from the out-of-work actors who man or woman it. The more advanced kiosks also invite passers-by to use the in-kiosk computer to enter the competition or to ask for more information about the kiosk holder's product.

Properly designed, maintained and manned, kiosks make attractive and possible potent additions to the outdoor advertising armoury.

Product dispensers in public places have some of the characteristics of kiosks. Coke, for instance, gain major publicity from its public dispensers – in offices, factories and canteens, for instance – even though most of the sales come through shops and supermarkets.

Literature   *RelModel Levels 1–5*

This category covers everything from a one-sided, one-colour leaflet to a multi-page, multi-coloured brochure, everything from a how-to-use-it technical explanation to an inspirational fanfare about a new holiday destination. It also includes catalogues, dealt with under a separate heading above.

Literature is just about the most flexible of all marketing and advertising media. You have complete control over content, style and cost. You can give it or send it to anyone you like, when and how you like. You can update it. You can run it as a one-off, or meld it into a larger campaign.

The rules governing good marketing literature are basically the same (the precise wording differs) as those governing every other kind of advertising and marketing communication, printed or electronic:

❏ You must know and understand your target both demographically and psychographically.

❏ The literature must make a single important, preferably unique and certainly persuasive claim ...

❏ ... and give the factual and emotional reasons why the claim is justified.

❏ You must decide the required reader response (what you want the reader to feel, think and do after reading the piece).

Magazines   *RelModel Levels 2–5*

This medium offers precise targeting. Whatever the age group you're targeting, whatever the occupation or profession, whatever the interest or hobby, whatever the type of person, there's a magazine, usually dozens, specially targeted at it, at her or at him. You should add, for completeness' sake, the magazines that appear with the daily and Sunday newspapers. The choice is overwhelming and the skills of the media specialist should be called in and used before you finalise your schedule.

The benefits of your advertisement being in the right magazine hardly need stating – but I will. For one thing, you can be sure that the readership is already attuned to your proposition, and the more specialist the magazine, the truer that is. The way that magazines are read makes it more likely that your advertisement will be seen and absorbed. Magazines, more often than not, are read at leisure, usually at home, often alone, or at least with only the family for company. Even business magazines are read at comparative leisure – in the chauffeur-driven limo for instance. Compare that with the way people read or try to read daily newspapers. Magazines also offer you good reproduction, but then so do most newspapers nowadays. Some magazines provide an 'advertiser's literature' service to readers, keying your advertisement to a pre-paid reply card. The publishers pass any requests for literature over to you. Product placement in targeted magazines is extremely powerful.

Mcomms (Mcommunications) *RelModel Levels 4–5*

Not so much media in their own right as ways of accessing other media. WAP mobiles, for instance, bring the Internet and much else to the palm of your hand. This is going to be a much-developed medium, as people increasingly demand services on the move. The General Motors Onstar initiative is a current example. With Onstar, you get not just a car but a whole set of security and personal on-the-move services – thanks to WAP technology. The crown-jewel prices paid by companies in the UK for the next generation of mobile phones shows how highly they prize a stake in WAP. Like interactive TV, this is one to watch.

Packaging *RelModel Levels 1–5*

Packaging has to work at the moment of truth, when the prospect's hand hovers over your product and then your competitors and then hopefully back to yours. So it must be attractive and impactful in its surface design and easy to pick up and hold. What is even more important is that it should reflect the image the consumer has in his/her mind. The packaging design and the whole appearance of the product should say: 'Hi, here's what you're looking for'. There's another vital point about packaging. It is the one piece of advertising that the consumer willingly takes away and displays in the home, the garage, the garden, wherever. Don't let it let you down. How many children, tomorrow's consumers, have grown familiar with a brand because they saw it week in week out on a shelf in the kitchen.

Point of sale   *RelModel Levels 1–5*

If packaging has to work at the moment of truth, point-of-sale material – in-store posters, shelf stickers, leaflets, perhaps in-store TV – has to work during the few seconds that precede it. The best point of sale crystallises all that the prospect has read, seen, heard or experienced of the product and gives a final nudge to buy. It has to reassure too, telling the prospect that all expectations aroused about the product can now be realised – like a mother showing her child the cycle she's been promising for weeks and saying: 'Look, it's just like I said it would be!'

Presentations   *RelModel Levels 3–5*

A presentation, for the purpose of this list, is the communication of a proposition to a comparatively small group of consumers or prospects or media who are there face to face with the presenter. Presentations can be made, still in real time, to people who are present only electronically, via teleconferencing. The same points apply.

The essence of a presentation is courtesy: 'what you are about to see and hear has been created specifically for you' – and that applies just as much to press conferences as to consumer presentations. Presentations on printed or hand-written charts were as effective as the presenter and his material. That remains true, but the advent of for example PowerPoint technology, where the material is computer-generated and presented, improves the quality of the images and consolidates the confidence of the presenter. Some simple rules need to be remembered: one overall proposition for the whole presentation; break down the proposition and its supporting evidence into bite size portions; start by telling the audience what you are going to tell them, then tell them, finally tell them what you've just told them. That way, you can't go wrong. Let people ask questions after but never during the presentation (that rule can be relaxed just a little if the presenter is feeling on top form – otherwise it's only too easy to lose the momentum of the presentation). Keep to 10 minutes for the presentation itself. Serve refreshments afterwards in the same or next door room and get your colleagues to join in the conversation. As the guests depart, give them a hard copy of the presentation. Two days later, send them a letter recapping briefly on the points made and asking if they need further elucidation.

Always try to be entertaining, engaging, always creative. Use techniques that keep people's attention – for instance, show special footage to illustrate what other people are saying about you or your product or service. Your aim is to surprise them. Your best response: 'Never thought of it in that way before. I'll buy it'.

Product placement   *RelModel Levels 3–5*

Cigarette manufacturers in the old days used to persuade the production companies to have their stars light a cigarette as often as possible during a movie – on the basis that the audience would follow suit. Getting your product into a big picture is still a worthwhile achievement particularly if the ambience is right. Rolls-Royce cars have enjoyed zillions of dollars of free publicity in films over the years. The ultimate, of course, is to sponsor whatever it is you want your product to appear in – then you can't be refused.

Public relations (PR)   *RelModel Levels 2–5*

Public relations, sometimes known more grandly as 'public affairs' or less grandly as 'press relations', are free at the point of reception by the target market, but expensive, demanding and time-consuming in the preparation. Your public relations are good when you are well spoken of in the media. Your public relations are good when whatever you claim in your advertising and other public statements is believed. Your public relations are good if, when your company makes a mistake, it is quickly forgiven. Your public relations are good when they reflect accurately the culture of your company. (What this means in practice is that if a journalist gets in conversation with one of your people in a pub, the answers he gets about the company harmonise with what he's just been told at last week's press conference.)

So how do you achieve this PR nirvana? The quick answer is to get a good public relations agency to work for you. But the answer the agency will give is the real answer: make sure that everything your company does is justifiable to the conscience of everyone working in the company. As Shakespeare made Polonius say to his son, Laertes as he was about to leave for the fleshpots of Paris:

This above all, to thine own self be true,
And it must follow, as the night the day,
Thou can'st not then be false to any man.

Translated into modern English that would make a good public relations motto, and one that should be observed by every member of the company, every member. It is the bedrock on which your public relations specialists can build some very imposing structures. Public relations without such a foundation collapse at the first sign of trouble. People are tired of spin; they want substance. The sad story of the Paddington train disaster at the end of 1999 illustrates the point. The public perception was that officials of the companies concerned were not being true to themselves and their responsibilities, and had not been for years before. The reputations of their companies are now in tatters and the best attempts of the public relations people are in vain.

But if honesty and openness are dominant, then public relations can do wonders for your products and your company as a whole. They can help launch brands and consolidate existing ones. They can help in recruitment. They can help the company when public approvals are needed for new construction on new sites, or for access to new markets or contracts here and overseas. In short, they can make the company and its contracts welcome.

Just as an aside: William Shakespeare was, by a kind of royal appointment, public relations consultant to the Tudor dynasty. His great series of history plays from Richard II to Henry VIII was a glorification of the Tudor monarchs and a denigration of the Plantagenets who preceded them. Popular history has taken Shakespeare's version as gospel. Richard III, for instance, has been remembered as a tyrant deservedly beaten by the saintly Henry VII, the first Tudor. Reality was not like that but public relations successfully obscured it. It doesn't often happen, mainly because you don't often have someone of Shakespeare's calibre on your PR staff.

Promotional items (give-aways, special offers, etc.)   *RelModel Levels 2–5*

People like something for nothing provided there's no catch. They're prepared to send off coupons, buy two rather than one, enter competitions, fill in questionnaires, even, in some cases, send off money to obtain the item you're offering. They're happy, of course, to get the item for free.

There's nothing too subtle about it. The item should be comparatively inexpensive to buy in quantity, should be of appropriate quality (no good giving away cutlery if it bends the first time it's used) and easy to display, dispatch, or include with the product being promoted. It can be relevant to the product or to the consumers and users. If it fits in with a longer-term marketing programme, and if you're lucky, you may hit upon a range of collectables. The never-known-to-fail collectables are glasses for long or short drinks. They're cheap to buy, can be made to look good and stylish, and people can't get too many, partly because they keep on breaking them. Pokémon-type figures have worked over the years for many different companies, not least the petrol companies. Tie-ups with a major sporting event – football, racing, etc. – are also good news.

The items should be branded, usually discreetly though you can go to the other extreme and blazon the product or company name over it – on a T-shirt for example.

Finally, don't make the mistake of making the item more popular than your funds will allow. Running out of promotional items is black mark no. 1. People have lost their jobs for it and for certain companies have lost consumers.

Radio   *RelModel Levels 2–5*

For many people this is the perfect partner, the perfect one-to-one experience, always available, goes everywhere with you, even on the morning run round the park, or stays at home with you, or in the car to and from work, undemanding unless you want it to be, involving if you like it, let's you get on with other things, talks to you, plays music, brings the news, and can be easily turned off. All that makes it an ideal marketing medium for practically any kind of product or service. With a good scriptwriter the medium's one major disadvantage – no visual – can be overcome. The pictures that words and music can create in the mind are often far better than those on the TV screen. It's also comparatively inexpensive. The commercials are cheap to make too.

Retail outlets   *RelModel Levels 1–5*

This is Centre Court. Win here, and you can't go far wrong. Lose, and you've wasted everything else you've worked for – unless you're an e-commerce company, in which case see the rest of this book.

The retail outlet, otherwise known as 'shop', 'store', 'supermarket', 'service station', 'kiosk', 'garden centre', 'hotel', 'bar', 'pub', 'bank', 'building society', 'estate agent', etc., is where individuals hand over money, either ready, paper or plastic, in exchange for products and services.

A retail outlet, particularly if it is on a high street, or part of a shopping centre, is economic democracy in action. The consumer has a very wide choice of product or service all within walking distance. The retailers and the manufacturers display their wares with every kind of explanation and persuasion, spoken, printed or electronic.

As a manufacturer and/or marketer, your responsibility is to see that the right goods with the right packaging and display support get to the right outlets at the right time. It is an enormously complex task and far beyond the scope of this book to treat – except to say that the 'All-to-One' principle applies here as everywhere else. The totality of the product or service must accord with the overall marketing proposition and the outlet's own environment and staff must be also in harmony. Consumers must recognise this totality. Their recognition will be subconscious, of course, but if anything in the mix is out of tune, they'll notice it, subconsciously or otherwise, and turn away.

The price of this 'retail outlet' democracy is competition. Everything about your product has to fit with the overall proposition, but it must also offer more to the chosen target market than competing products do. It must also attract the passing trade, the uncommitted, the browsers, the impulse buyers. It must also attract those who are not in the market on that occasion for your type of product – they are the potential next-time buyers.

The retail outlet is the Centre Court. It is also the court of last appeal. Make sure your product or service appeals in the right way.

Roadside posters   *RelModel Levels 1–5*

Essentially there are two kinds: billboards on the main roads or smaller boards in the shopping centres. The main road sites are usually used for long-term campaigns putting across a name, a personality and a proposition. The shopping centre boards can do the same job. They can also be used for last-minute reminders. The prospects are on the way to the shops. The board is one of your last chances to remind them of your brand (point of sale is the very last).

'All-to-One' applies here too. Everything about the poster must carry the same essential message and convey the same personality, as does every other medium.

Sales and service representatives   *RelModel Levels 2–5*

A good sales representative is the third-best advertising medium. The service representative is the second best but still very powerful, especially if he/she turns up in an emergency. Only word-of-mouth recommendation by friends and neighbours can beat either.

The usual requirements apply. Representatives must project the overall proposition and demonstrate the courtesy, consideration and commitment implicit in every good proposition. They need first-class training and regular refresher courses. And because they are often working alone, they need to be fully committed to the company and its products and services.

Sales reps are high cost, but they are highly interactive (responding on the spot to a prospective consumer's questions and worries) and so can produce a high level of returns. They can distribute product, be (politely) intrusive, seek out prospects, follow the process right from awareness to transaction and consumer loyalty. And because they are considerate and sensitive to the prospect's needs, they can also cross sell – 'I came to talk about your washing machine, but since you mention it, we do a very efficient drier.' Sorted!

Signage   *RelModel Levels 1–5*

Think of your company as a person and you'll want it to be suitably dressed at all times. Signage, a short-hand term for the appearance of all your installations – stores, offices, factories, depots, everything – is about how your company is dressed. Signage should be a key part of the company's visible manifestations (VM) and should play a key role in the way the company portrays itself. In other words it is a key part of the holistic 'All-to-One' concept, and at its most effective, the signage will reassure a consumer or prospect that all's well with the company and that everything about the company contributes to the level of service and product quality provided to consumers. It's that important.

Let me give you one example. Until two or three years ago the Lever Brothers plant at Warrington looked – how shall I say – very unLeverish. Levers make and sell products that make you look clean, feel good and smell better. From the outside, this plant conveyed none of those ideas. Yet it is directly adjacent to the railway station on the main line to the Borders and Scotland. Any individual consumer or supermarket buyer travelling north must have had one or two critical thoughts as the train waited at the station. Today, I'm glad to say it's been given a makeover. But not before time.

Sports sponsorship   *RelModel Levels 2–5*

Unless you're content with the local bowls contest, you're talking very big money with sports sponsorship. Only you and your specialist advisers can decide whether the investment will produce adequate dividends. The dividends, of course, can be enormous. Your company and its brands are completely integrated into the programme content – you can't be zapped out or otherwise ignored. You're part of the enjoyment – and given some of the credit for creating it. Your name is linked with the hero-gods of the sports field and the glamorous lifestyle they project, and repeated non-stop in the media. The sport you sponsor can have direct links with your company and products – a high-tech brand will benefit from links with motor-sports for instance. You often have a multinational audience. The PR can be enormous. And the occasion offers your sales people wonderful opportunities to meet clients and prospects on very favourable terms in a motivating environment.

At the moment, it's difficult to measure the direct selling effectiveness of sponsorship, although the media coverage that results from it can be measured reasonably accurately to give you some idea of how well the money was spent. Sponsorship has enjoyed double digit growth for at least 10 years, today accounting for $23 billion of the marketing spend. While it was previously acceptable that sponsorship deals happened on the chairman's whim, today the size of the industry means that at least the higher-end is under heavy pressure to 'grow up' and offer more measurability and accountability. While the jury is out, hotly debating what elements need to be evaluated in order to reach qualitative answers, media coverage is about the only effect of sponsorship on which there is a degree of consensus. Everybody agrees it is a fundamental goal of sponsorship, there is rough agreement on the methods of measuring it and sponsorship-monitoring companies have proliferated.

Staff uniforms   *RelModel Levels 1–5*

Uniforms mean pride in your role and commitment to your responsibilities. They also save your own clothes from wear. So uniforms are a good thing – provided they are well designed and provided the staff think they're well designed. Consumers like them for those first two reasons. They like being served by people who take pride in their work and are committed to their responsibilities. They also like to recognise immediately the people they can talk to and get help from.

Uniforms have another benefit. They bring out the best in people. The spirit of the regiment lives on!

Stationery   *RelModel Levels 1–5*

Stationery – one-off letters (as distinct from a direct mail) and even invoices – is magnificently intrusive. It goes straight to the person addressed who is prepared to open and read it because it contains a unique message specially written for his/her eyes. The stationery design should reflect other aspects of the company – its so-called visual manifestations. A letter, even an invoice, addressed to the individual consumer, represents the company in a rather special way. It must reflect the company's personality.

Sunday newspapers   *RelModel Levels 1–5*

The big difference from daily newspapers is the day. People in the West still treat Sunday as somewhat different. Sunday newspapers tend to stay in the home (dailies are often taken by people going out to work). They are read in a relaxed environment. And they are enormous, so your advertisements possibly have to work even harder to win the attention you want.

Supermarket floors   *RelModel Levels 3–5*

Advertising on any kind of shop floor can remind people of a name, pack or slogan. It's really point of sale, but its effectiveness is difficult to measure. It's a useful addition if you've money to spare. But be aware of the symbolism of having your name trodden under foot.

Telephones   *RelModel Levels 4–5*
including WAPs/mobiles

Highly interactive, very personal, potentially powerful and completely private, even more private than the web. Requirements for success are a reliable database, eYcient selection and, above all, a well-trained high-morale staV at the centre. DiYcult as it is, the staV must be able to project the company's personality/proposition in their voice and the manner and content of their pitch and in their responses to consumer questions.

Teletext   *RelModel Levels 3–5*

Teletext was the nearest thing to the Internet before the Internet came along, in the sense that the words and rather peculiar graphics came up on the screen in response to pressing a few buttons. To many, Teletext might seem a very minor medium. But it reaches people when they are in a relaxed mood – it's not intrusive. And its gentle reminders of product names and attributes can trigger positive purchase intentions. It has a great track record in the holiday market where its last-minute news facility put it hours ahead of the press – but that was when it was more of a novelty than it is today.

Teletext was the forerunner of interactive TV. It has helped to get people used to the idea of accessing information and sales messages from their TV screen.

Tickets   *RelModel Levels 1–5*

Your company or brand name on the back of a ticket is a reminder – not much more. If the ticket is to a prestigious event, or at least one that your prospect finds particularly interesting, then there is some kudos to be gained.

TV   *RelModel Levels 1–5*

This remains the most powerful medium. Nothing else offers the same range of benefits: viewers of all ages, of all socio-economic groups, of all educational backgrounds, at any time of the day or night, can choose from an almost endless choice of entertainment, news, instruction and education. The medium dominates the home; every household has at least one set. TV complements the lifestyle of the whole family and varies with it. For much of the day TV is the centre of family life, but individuals alone can also enjoy it. During the day it gives the children something to think about and keeps grandma amused. On great occasions it takes on almost a religious significance. Constant technological improvements – cable, satellite, digital, big screen and now interaction – give it contemporaneity. It can be a very selective medium – thanks to the choice of channels now available and the range of audiences attracted at off-peak times. At peak times, the reach remains extremely high, although channel-hopping can make viewership figures unreliable. With TV, you get reach when you need it, selectivity when you want it, and as much frequency as you can afford.

The advertising carried within the TV context takes authority and acceptance from it. But high production values are needed. The second rate can't compete. No other medium allows such effective product demonstration or such convincing celebrity endorsement. No other medium allows you to make such powerful straight-from-the-shoulder sales pitch. No other medium allows you to create such pervasive 'images'. No other medium catches people in such a relaxed, receptive, confident frame of mind.

There's more. If your commercials are up to it, you can create national legends. People watch out for the next in a series to find out what happens to the heroine (even though she only gets a second cup of coffee). In fact the leverage can be very effective, with spin-offs that can include fashionwear, music chart-toppers and even books. (British Telecom reprinted the storyboards of one series of TV commercials in book form and actually sold them.)

You can also exploit pester power – although you really shouldn't. 'Pester power' is what children apply to their parents and other amenable adults. It consists of a series of repeated requests, accompanied ad lib by winsome smiles or whining references to the next door's children and how much better treated they are, for a certain product seen advertised mainly on TV. You should not encourage this, particularly if you are selling confectionery or, at Christmas time, toys. But encouraged or not, it happens and is another sign of the power of TV.

Vehicle livery   *RelModel Levels 1–5*

Your vehicles are moving poster sites, moving visiting cards, roving ambassadors. I once knew a chairman who cancelled a valuable contract with one supplier because one of their trucks cut him up on the motorway. That'll learn 'em. Good manners from your drivers is as important as good manners from your sales staff – more and more companies are realising that nowadays, and about time too.

Vehicle livery along with staff uniforms, signage and stationery present the company to the public every minute of every day and in every part of the country. They are among the most visible of the visible manifestations. No driver on UK roads can be unfamiliar with Eddie Stobart and his endless stream of trucks carrying his name and his energetic promise of express road haulage.

Your vehicle livery scheme, as far as feasible, will project your company's personality and style and will therefore work synergistically with every other business communication.

Video/DVD   *RelModel Levels 4–5*

A few years back, when video was still a novelty, it was fashionable to offer one to prospective purchasers of conservatories, holidays, and such like, even computers. It's still done, but today the main use of video and DVD is for business-to-business presentation, where they can be very effective if a little inflexible and more than a little expensive.

DVD, by the way, stands for digital versatile disc or digital video disc (take your pick). It's like a CD but with much more capacity, offering video as well as sound. It is now beginning to replace tape video because it offers higher quality and more reliability. It also offers immense flexibility in use – you can click/flick backwards and forwards at will, perfect for presentations.

Wall charts   *RelModel Levels 3–5*

Wall charts are a kind of forgotten medium. Even when they're up on the wall, they're somehow taken for granted. This, of course, is their real strength. No one feels pressurised by a wall chart and they're useful for covering up stains and holes.

They're great for children (sporting events and pop stars) and for enthusiasts of every kind. The charts will get pinned up somewhere, and probably stay where they are pinned indefinitely. They're good in a business-to-business environment. They'll often do a better job than the company calendar (though I'll never knock a company calendar that gets put up, and most of them are).

Wall charts can carry plenty of useful text, but they need a strong visual element, and they must have the stamina both in subject and material to last. A good wall chart is your permanent representative.

Word of mouth   *RelModel Levels 1–5*

Word of mouth is the oldest communication medium known to man (and woman) – if you exclude digital communication in its original meaning of giving information or opinions with the fingers.

No amount of money spent in the public media will avail if the word of mouth is against you. It's a medium you can't buy into directly, but it's one which the propagandists and spin-doctors are constantly aiming to reach.

Word-of-mouth recommendation or denigration comes mainly from someone's direct experience of a product or service, tempered by the aura created through the advertising and marketing generally, though the experience will dominate. Sometimes, of course, the experience is second, third or umpteenth hand. The recipient of the advice has to make a judgement on how reliable the opinion is. The manufacturer has no control except to make sure that people's experience of the products and services is good.

There are, however, some techniques that can be applied. Here are two. The first is 'the joke anyone can repeat without messing it up'. Politicians and their spinners have long been adept at making up jokes which 'ordinary' people can appreciate and, better still, can pass on. One good joke (I won't mention the victim, although he was a major politician) had it that the person in question was so wet he tucked his shirt into his underpants. It's the kind of crack that any would-be wit can repeat in the pub without getting it wrong. It did enormous damage and at no cost to the party that first put it about.

The second is the one-liner. Take, for instance: 'Nobody got fired for buying IBM', a line that the company was only too happy to nourish and propagate. I daren't think how many times that line has been trotted out to justify play-safe policies. But, in its heyday, it helped make millions for Big Blue. More recently think of 'Vorsprung durch technik'. The line, repeated over and over again in every kind of context, did wonders for Audi.

One-liners in support of your business are good to have and you can have some control over them. But the most powerful word of mouth – and there's a lot of it about – is the impromptu over-the-fence, round-the-table, in-the-pub remark from a respected friend. You know the kind of thing: 'That car (brand mentioned) has been a pain in the neck since I got it' or 'It's the best buy we've ever made' or 'Don't believe a word they tell you' and so on indefinitely. Word of mouth can make you or destroy you. And once the word has got around, it can take you forever to change it. For most of the last century, Ford in the UK had a cheap and cheerful image, names like 'Ford Popular' contributing (it was a great car and a collectors' favourite now), not to mention jokes such as 'any colour so long as it's black'. Advertising, promotions, motor-racing successes and, above all, style and manufacturing quality have redeemed the situation, but it has taken decades!

Richard Branson is quoted as saying: 'When we launched Virgin Direct (Virgin financial sector company) we found word of mouth,

The importance of demographic versus psychographic

Demographic information is objectively factual, can be stored and later understood by anyone without risk of ambiguity. On the other hand, lifestyle information, otherwise known as psychographic information, tends to be subjective and is more susceptible to uncertainty. For instance: the answer to 'what is your marital status?', is a provable demographic fact – give or take the odd joke. But, for instance, a preference for foreign cheeses is a psychographic fact and one that varies in significance with different people (I like Camembert, you adore Camembert, she would die for Camembert). In any case the very existence of a psychographic fact depends on the consumer saying so, which he/ she might have said simply because it sounded good at the time. Behavioural information has the same characteristics.

Nevertheless, lifestyle, behavioural and all such psychographic information is immensely valuable in fine-tuning the details of a strategic marketing campaign or a particular component of the campaign. It is also essential if your marketing activity is to have the decisive impact and influence on the target consumers that overall success demands. In real life, it is also a fact that creative people are inspired by psychographics, numbed by demographics. Psychographic information is a necessary precursor of great advertising.

fuelled by a small public relations campaign, was more than 30 times as effective as the small amount we spent on advertising.' Beat that.

Now make your own assessment

The above media assessments, including the RelModel scoring, are mine – nothing scientific about them! You clearly will have your own assessments, but I doubt whether they will be substantially different, even though they will be as subjective as mine. Actually, the number of objective facts about media is very small. Its format is an objective fact, so is the price you pay to appear in it and the price its readership/viewership pays, if any, to access it. With print, you have the objective fact of circulation and distribution. With electronic media, there is the objective fact of the number of people who could possibly access it. And, of course, access to a medium means only that! Every other criterion on which to judge a medium's suitability is subjective.

The final media point, and potentially the killer, is that the best media mix is of no avail if the quality of the message you want to project is inadequate. However high-tech the medium, it must still be human talking to human and in the most persuasive way possible.

Admirantys

Close-focusing on the client and the consumers

I T'S THE AGE-OLD question: how do you measure the advertising value of sponsorship? Easy, if you're a client of Admirantys, an international company with offices in the UK and the USA. Thanks to some dazzling new technology, Admirantys, through its Captimax service, can convert sponsorship investment in fast-moving events, such as motor-sport, horse-racing, bob-sleigh racing, aerobatics, downhill skiing, into measurable TV impacts, capable of being codified in a rate card. Simple as that!

It's a classic example of how to create a business by first getting close to the client and the consumer, finding out what they want, and then producing the technology that delivers what they want.

Clients of the Captimax service are the sponsors. They want measurable impacts from their investment – and not just a chance to chat up the stars. In short, they want measurable TVRs (TV ratings) and in the past they just weren't getting them. So far as the consumers are concerned, especially the fans who watch on TV, they want to feel part of the action, to get fully focused pictures of everything throughout, not the usual blurred shots of the crowd, the scenery and the occasional streaking competitors.

The Captimax answer to both sets of requirements is a brilliant technological breakthrough, a camera-based piece of wizardry called Navicam. This is how it works. The client logo appears on every competitor – car, horse, skier, whatever. The Navicam system provides intelligent control of the cameras. The system knows at all times the precise position of all the 'targets' (the competitors to be filmed) – so it always has the most relevant action, including the unexpected, in close focus and captures it all without fail.

All this is a massive improvement for any sports viewer. For sponsors, it means that their brand identification can always be in rock-steady focus, whatever the speed of the competitors, and whether the aim is to maintain a balanced view of the whole event or

Case study (continued)

to give selective coverage. The Navicam technology is infinitely better than human hands at locking onto the target throughout any kind of action shot. Again, this gives viewers better pictures and a keener feeling of presence. It also gives sponsors sharp, steady, continuous exposure for their brands throughout.

There's more. Sponsors know before the event how many minutes of exposure they're going to get – and they can confirm the number after the event in playback. They also know how many people watched the event on TV. So – they have the TVRs they need. QED.

What's in it for the fans? Only the best TV pictures ever. They miss nothing of the action. And everything is in clear sharp focus. None of this would have happened, if Admirantys hadn't first focused closely on their prospective clients and consumers. They did, and it happened. Admirantys believe that it has created a new medium. And, not surprisingly perhaps, it calls this new medium: 'Close-focus' sponsorship. It's a winner.

Hype, heresy, hoax

HYPE ABOUT THE Internet is set to become the marketing heresy of our time (perhaps hoax is more accurate) – and no one has publicly admitted it, certainly no one has written a book admitting it. Perhaps no one has realised it. They will. They will. Even the dotcoms will come to realise it, hopefully before they go bust (for some it's already too late).

Like all heresies (or hoaxes), the hype grossly over-emphasises one aspect of the truth, in this case, the immense and exciting importance of the Internet as a marketing tool, and pooh-poohs all other marketing tools including all other media and 'conventional' marketing tenets.

The happy fact is that, whatever the technology, however fascinating, persuasive and invasive, the people who use it don't change. They remain what they always were. And they were never screen-bound nerds sitting at a desk thrilled to be having indefinite one-to-one electronic relationships with strangers. What they want now, is what they've always wanted – variety, difference, abundance and fresh air. Of course, they want to be treated as unique individuals ('One-to-One' is on target there), but they like to have dealings with more than one person and in more than one communication medium (there's more to life than being glued to a screen). Sometimes, quite often in fact, people rather like being part of a group. Ever so often, they quite enjoy being interrupted. 'One-to-One', mould breaking though it was in its time, fails to recognise any of those vital human instincts.

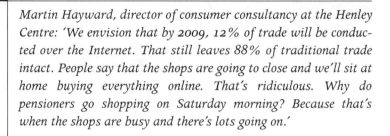

*Martin Hayward, director of consumer consultancy at the Henley
Centre: 'We envision that by 2009, 12% of trade will be conducted over the Internet. That still leaves 88% of traditional trade
intact. People say that the shops are going to close and we'll sit at
home buying everything online. That's ridiculous. Why do
pensioners go shopping on Saturday morning? Because that's
when the shops are busy and there's lots going on.'*

Consumers want more than the Internet. They want better-quality
interaction with companies, better-quality interaction than the
Internet can provide.

Anyone engaged in consumer marketing at any level knows from
daily experience that the Internet is only one aspect of marketing
truth (though an increasingly significant one), that it can only be
part of the overall effort, that it is not the be-all and end-all of business, that marketing is not simply a limited one-to-one experience
(especially if one of them communicates only through a screen).

Consumers prefer, no, insist on, communicating with whoever we
want to communicate with in whatever way suits us when we are
buying something or selling something, or just going about our daily
lives. The truth is that marketing is an all-company responsibility,
not something that only the online experts know about ... that
marketing is as many-sided as life and that there's more to life than
staring at a screen while you fiddle with a keyboard.

There's worse yet. Under the influence of the 'One-to-One'
concept, consumer relationship marketing (CRM), that dazzlingly
effective aid to long-term business success, was in danger of becoming two-dimensional. Worse still, the very dazzle of the concept and
its Internet expression has blinded companies to those fundamental
marketing truths and practices which remain the only sure
guarantees of business success.

Anyone engaged in the day-to-day business of living, knows that
people, even the most besotted of Internetters, have a thousand and

> *More than 60 per cent of online shoppers abandon their (virtual) shopping cart or leave their purchase forms uncompleted. (Forrester)*

one things to do that they can't do (except with great difficulty) when they are staring at a screen with fingers on the keyboard. Most human requirements, commercial or otherwise, simply cannot be delivered, experienced, let alone enjoyed through a screen. The warm multidimensional relationship of the corner-shop (for instance) simply cannot be achieved when the only means of contact is via umpteen miles of glass fibre.

Am I exaggerating? If I am, it's worth doing so to make the point. Some writers of books about the Internet give the impression that it's hardly possible to exaggerate the future role of the Internet. They seem overwhelmed to the point of being disconnected from reality. People are not.

The Internet today is more or less taken for granted. Everyone's auntie is online. Even the children are getting blasé, at least the brighter ones are. Consumers in the new Internet-plus economy now emerging are no longer electronically naïve and they are underwhelmed by the Internet (dotcom failures haven't helped). As a result, even those marketers hardest bitten by the Internet bug are once again seeing the attraction of the full range of media (the buying public never lost sight of it).

They will continue to live their lives more or less as they always have. They may spend more time inter-reacting with the Internet and less time sitting passively in front of a TV screen, through which they will also, of course, be able to interact with the Internet. WAP technology will put the Internet in everyone's hands wherever they go, peering through specially provided super-magnifying spectacles at that tiny, tiny screen before falling down a manhole probably.

But there will still remain only 24 hours in the day. How many of those will people spend online? You can imagine some enthusiasts on some days spending all or nearly all their waking hours visiting one website or another. The fact is that as of now, the average time spent on the Internet by those with the capability, is approximately 45 minutes a day, just over 3 per cent. Will it increase? It may, it probably will, but by how much? For the foreseeable future, ordinary human need for the warmth of real companionship, friendship and love, for fresh air, for the touch, feel and smell of things, for the sheer variety of life, all that will keep the Internet firmly in its place, as yet another wonderful and different means of communication to add to those already available.

What is certain is that today's most successful marketers know how to use the Internet for what it is, a valuable tool and an indispensable component in the overall marketing mix. The best companies are using the Internet with increasing effectiveness but only as part of their overall interaction with their consumers, actual and potential, their involvement in the real life of the people they want to influence and do business with on a lifelong basis. To such companies 'All-to-One' is the consumer relationship, the one most likely to deliver sustainable growth and profitability. For them, that is what it is delivering now.

The key point I want to make is that in 'All-to-One' marketing, the Internet is no more than a part of the 'All'.

But an extremely important part! The Internet as a communication medium has already achieved an immeasurably faster growth rate than any other new medium. Even television, the champion of champions until the Internet arrived, took decades to reach its present eminence. The Internet has taken months.

Successful companies are exploiting the superlative and unique advantages of the Internet while avoiding the potentially devastating drawbacks. Above all, and this is the essence of the book's message, the Internet can be used synergistically as part of an overall communication/selling dialogue with all the different types of audience that need to be reached and attracted if the company and its products and services are to have a long-term, profitable future.

Because of the immediacy of the Internet, its speed and flexibility, it allows companies to experiment with different product ideas, different product propositions and different promotional approaches to different consumer segments for comparative peanuts, certainly when compared with the cost of carrying out similar exercises in other media. For that alone it is able to give powerful and unique assistance in the whole 'ideas to implementation' process, a process that lies at the heart of all successful business.

Perhaps it's too much to expect, but it would be good all round if anyone still brave enough to set up a dotcom were to take time off to read this book first. A mountain of problems and the accompanying newspaper headlines would be avoided. If the dotcom already exists and that mountain is lurking round the next bend, then the book could still throw a lifeline. Dotcoms go down usually because they are too poorly structured and managed. The book can show them the better way.

I want the Internet to be seen and treated as just another medium, vast, far-reaching, wonderful, powerful, all that and more, but just another medium. Use it for what it can give you and for its synergy with other media. But don't lose your way in the cloud of hyperbole that currently surrounds it.

In short I want to cut hype, lose the heresy, and put in place instead a genuine culture change. We need to take a holistic view of the marketing tools available to us and everybody in the company must subscribe to that view and act on it. The Internet is a magnificent marketing tool, but it's far from being the only one. It will work better for all of us when we use it as part of our total marketing approach.

Uncontrolled! Uncontrollable?

You can and should wax lyrical about the Internet as a superb manifestation of the free spirit. No one controls it. No one is barred. Entry costs are virtually non-existent — once the basics have been bought, and their cost comes down almost daily.

However, with human beings being what they are, there will always be someone calling the Internet a 'free-for-all', another refusing to give credit card details for fear of being robbed, someone else asking for censorship, another showing signs of nervousness because it can't be controlled, someone else saying it's the world's worst time-waster, especially for kids, yet another condemning it as a pornographers' paradise.

Is that the kind of language you like to hear about a medium where your product and company feature strongly?

For marketers jealous of their product and company images, there must always be a question mark over the Internet's public reputation. To entrust those images only to the Internet is to put them at risk. They need buttressing from the outside.

The on-going technological revolution

B ILL GATES SAID it: 'Most people overestimate what is going to happen in two years and underestimate what is going to happen in 10 years.'

Futurology has never been an exact science, not even an exact crystal ball. I'll hazard one guess though: no technological breakthrough will come to anything, unless people believe that it helps them enjoy their lives more. In other words, technological wizardry for its own sake won't last. What we can do in this section, is to list the technological possibilities. It's always good to know what may happen. Some of the possibilities have a future and some of the prophecies will come true. I'll indicate those I think have staying power.

❏ A decade ago, early Internet users worked at data speeds of 2.4K. They could send and receive short text messages. Today, the average home phone line supports calls of up to 56K, still well short of the speed needed to access CD-quality audio let alone the full-screen video quality modern PCs can handle. A new technology appears in 2000 called ADSL (Asymmetric Digital Subscriber Line). It brings broadband access without the need for rewiring. The next fastest technology is ISDN. ADSL starts at a speed of 512K and will accelerate over the years. It will allow a constant stream of digital information covering everything from

video calls from around the world to interactive TV and
downloadable digital music CDs. Its speed will allow subscribers
to use software from an ASP (applications service provider).

❑ 200 million people throughout the world will be on the Internet
by the end of 2000 – 500 million two years later.

❑ Nearly 60 per cent of the world's population will be online in
2005.

❑ In 1998, total value of e-business was $2.5 billion. In 2000, it was
$510 billion give or take. So in five years it could be – who
knows?

❑ Call centres, banks, utilities, retail chains and a growing number
of smaller businesses are now enjoying the benefits of CRM
software, some as a result of direct purchase, some by
outsourcing. The market for it has grown accordingly. In 1994, it
was worth $200 million. In 2000 the value is $3 billion, which is
predicted to grow to over $8 billion in a couple of years.

❑ The era of PC dominance is coming to an end – though the
number of PCs will continue to grow to 600 million within two
years.

❑ The next two years will see increasingly sophisticated mobile
communications (stemming from the introduction of WAP –
wireless application protocol – technology).

❑ There will be embedded computational technology linked to the
Internet in household appliances and any other appliance you can
think of. The technology is already on the market. It's low cost
and needs little power and communicates via radio transmission.
No wires, no cables.

❑ Television set-top boxes allow interactive TV and e-mail via the
Internet.

❑ The computing power available to individuals will continue to
double every 18 months.

❏ Bandwidth, thanks in part to the introduction of glass fibre, will triple every year – to make e-mail and the Internet faster, more reliable. Glass fibre has quite incredible capacity – all the telephone conversations made in the USA on any one day can be carried on a single glass fibre the size of a human hair.

❏ In 1996, all access to the Internet was through PCs. In two years, more than half of all Internet access will be through other devices, including TV and WAP.

❏ Over half the UK population already have mobile phones.

❏ In five years, there will be 1 billion mobile phone users throughout the world, and nearly two-thirds of their phones will be WAP enabled. Wireless technology will enable portable devices such as the aforesaid mobile phones as well as laptop computers and PDAs (personal digital assistants, i.e. even smaller computers). E-mail, Internet and conversation opportunities will all be on hand – literally. So-called third generation (3G) mobile devices we are told will increase data speeds from 384,000 bps (bits per second) to 2,000,000 bps. Add to that the promised improvement in processing power, and everyone's mobile becomes a workable multimedia machine.

The big advantages are obvious. People will be able to find out what's on at the cinema, whether seats are available, do the booking, be told how to get there and where to park. People will be able to hold video conferences while on the move. You'll be able to surf the Net wherever you are.

I'm all for all that. But I think the overall message from all this new technology, actual and potential is that the 'All-to-One' approach to business in general and marketing in particular will become easier to achieve. 'One-to-one' began with the introduction of the Internet – although, as I've said elsewhere in this book, it fails to exploit the full potential. The new personal, mobile communication devices make 'All-to-One' even more the natural way to do business with everybody.

A quick word on CRM applications software

CRM applications software is a generic name for the back-office consumer-account packages. These powerful tools enable consumer-service agents to see at a glance an individual's history as a consumer. So when a consumer is contacted, he or she will not be troubled with an irrelevant sales pitch but offered a product or service tailored to the individual's needs, in theory at least. CRM software is sophisticated enough to store all kinds of details about a consumer's spending habits — information culled from loyalty cards, past purchases and responses to previous offers. These data can be matched with personal details such as age, sex, address, educational background, hobbies and interests, job/position/ profession and match all that in with market research information. Data-mining and consumer prioritisation enable companies to calculate how much an individual's business is worth to them over the long term, even a lifetime. The criterion of competitive success then becomes not 'what share of market have we won' but 'what share of an individual's entire lifetime purchasing in our product/service area have we won'. And, again by the way, once you start thinking of consumers enjoying a lifelong relationship with you, you start to ask yourself 'just what product are we making'. Ford, as keen as anyone on the lifetime consumer, think of themselves now not as car makers but as mobility suppliers which sounds a bit odd but which describes far more accurately their role as providers of trouble-free personal transport for life. This kind of thinking comes naturally when the CRM is up and running.

CRM and today's software

The information stored and assembled by CRM software could come from a variety of sources – including loyalty cards, all past transactions (hence buying habits), responses to previous offers, consumer calls of every description plus generally available market research or research commissioned by your company. The more different sources for the information, the better. Information about a consumer is far more valuable when it comes from a variety of sources, in and out of the company.

Fed into the CRM system, this 'behavioural' information is matched with factual personal details – age, sex, marital status, address, occupation, etc. – to give a profile of each consumer. You can then segment your market and target each segment with full knowledge of its size, characteristics and buying propensities. You can prioritise the segments, identifying those that offer the most valuable business (high-value consumers) and on a lifetime basis. Moreover, you can shed unprofitable segments. And because you know your consumers 'in the round', and can more precisely predict their likely reactions, you can react more quickly and positively when basic shifts in consumer behaviour and attitude impinge on the company/consumer relationship.

CRM is the basis on which to build an 'All-to-One' enterprise.

A vision of what might be

T HE PROVERB SAYS that 'where there is no vision the people perish'. Substitute 'business' for 'people' and add 'es' to 'perish' and you've summed up this section. One recent US President called it 'this vision thing'. You can't run a business or your life without it. It's all to do with being human – flesh, blood, imagination, passions, phobias, memories, all that kind of thing – and not robots, so many Mr Spocks, responding logically and inevitably to logical arguments. Of course, you can't defy logic, at least not for long. Logic is the entry fee for practically everything (guess the exceptions), but if you want to get anywhere in business as in life, you usually have to go beyond logic, beyond but not on the bypass. The RelModel takes full account of that fact. It shows you the practical, logical things you have to do, then allows you, encourages you, *forces* you to use your creativity, bright ideas, instincts, brainwaves, insights, vision – call it what you like so long as it embraces logic before going beyond it. Mediaeval alchemists tried to turn base metals into gold. They failed. Vision, provided it is based on logic, usually does the trick.

In your business, with the help of this vision thing, you can jump from the well thought-out but ordinary to the well thought-out and extra-ordinary, and it's the extra-ordinary that has the potential of generating the most long-term value from each consumer. This jump is needed as much in company organisation and people handling as it is in decisions about marketing and marketing communications. But to describe what jump you have to make in any particular situation is like trying to describe an elephant. Who cares how you describe it? If one came into the room right now, you'd have no difficulty in recognising it.

It's the same with the jump! If I told you that 'British Airways carries more paying international passengers than any other airline in the world', you might be impressed, you might be inclined to give them a go, you might be inclined to think that the claim is an empty boast, or you might think 'so what?'. If I told you that 'British Airways is the world's favourite airline', you would, I suggest, feel just a little warmer towards it and even more inclined to choose it when you next had a choice. Moreover, you'd remember it. Both statements are based on the same information and are essentially saying the same thing. The second says it with the benefit of vision. As a result it's a winner.

You can make the same comparison with any worthwhile advertising idea. Microsoft's 'Where do you want to go today?' is based on the proposition that via Microsoft you can be connected to any part of the world. But don't the right words in the right order make a difference. The word 'poetry' comes to mind.

'Because I'm worth it' contains a love letter of meaning for the woman watching a L'Oréal TV commercial, and says in four words far more than the thousands of words in the research documents which reported with copious evidence that women who care about their looks will pay more for their cosmetics.

Another simple example I've been told about – it was long before my time – concerns Shell in the UK and Shell in the USA. Both companies, or rather subsidiaries of the companies were selling exactly the same product, a strip containing a slow-release pesticide, called Vapona. Hung up in the home or pigsty or stable or wherever, the strip killed all flying insects in the neighbourhood (the product incidentally has now been withdrawn). The Shell company in the UK launched it under the brand name, Vapona Pest Strip. What could be more straightforward? The US company launched it under the name, Vapona No-Pest Strip. What could be more true? Both launches did

Great ideas are obvious once someone points them out. The classic example has Christopher Columbus of all people boasting that he could make an egg stand on its end every time, without fail, no rolling about. But before demonstrating his skill, he challenged his friends to do the trick. They couldn't. 'Come on, Chris,' they shouted, 'show us'. Christopher took an egg, took a spoon, and gently tapped the end of the egg to form a safe base, and the egg stood firm. 'Voila', he said in Italian. The friends were furious. 'If we'd known that, we could have done it', they cried. QED.

well, but one did very, very well indeed. The addition of that little word 'no' is a magnificent example of a successful creative jump.

One characteristic of a successful jump is that it's soon taken for granted. The extra-ordinary soon seems the most natural thing in the world, so obviously the right thing. Take Richard Branson and his Virgin brand again. The creative jump there was to use Branson himself as the brand icon. Today it seems the most natural thing in the world. But he could, I suppose, have run his companies without his name, face or figure featuring at all. Perhaps his early business advisers — if he had any — advised against any suspicion of a personality cult. 'Look at Freddie Laker', they might have said. He started a airline with his face everywhere, and look what happened to him?' Or they might have said: 'People like to think they're flying with a large organisation full of strong quiet professionals.' They could have been right, but in Branson's case they weren't. Branson and his personality with all that it means in terms of youth (how old is he now?), adventure and irreverence are now an intrinsic part of the Virgin brand.

Which is a cue to remind us all that the jump involves risk. You might jump the wrong way, or not far enough, or too far. But without the jump you won't get anywhere.

You must encourage everyone in the company to take that risk. They will do it if you show them the vision of what might be, the clear way ahead (and provide something for them to fall back on!).

Eight

Image rules ... brand stays king

IMAGE IS SOMETHING everything and everybody has and can't escape from. It is the most important thing about her, him and it, and it exists only in the head (so it's intangible). Each of our heads contains a near infinity of different images of people and things. We have an image of everyone we know, everything we use, and everything we see, hear, smell and touch as we go about living our lives. Each image is the result of our relation with that person or thing over time, an amalgam of everything we have known, experienced, thought, read, heard and seen about that person or thing. It is yet another example of the universality of the 'All-to-One' construct. Humans love that construct. They live by it! So people hate being short-changed, when someone or something they have come to like and respect reveals aspects which are not likeable and not worthy of respect. Image is 'All' or it is nothing.

In business, the 'All' contributing to the one image of a product or company includes: experience of the product/company; other people's reporting of *their* experience; the advertising and promotion generally; the point-of-sale environment; mentions in the media; competitive activity; and the hard competitive facts about the product/company itself (usually last in the queue). But images are not carved out of stone. They need non-stop doses of that tender loving care we were talking about earlier – which means that the company and its products must continue to deliver on their promises, that the promises must be consistent with consumer requirements, and changing consumer requirements, which in turn means that the company's culture should remain consumer-centred in every detail.

The image itself must remain unchanged, or apparently unchanged. Images must change in line with changing tastes, but not so as people notice. People like products whose image remains familiar to them. They can be intrigued by products whose image is entirely new. What they will not tolerate is an image that looks familiar at a quick first glance, but on a moment's extra look is obviously wrong. People hate that. Here's an example. Which packet of cornflakes would you be most likely to pick up from a supermarket shelf? One with the words John Smith's Cornflakes and a straightforward picture of corn or one with the words Kelogs Cornflakes and a design that nearly but not quite looks like the real thing. You'd probably avoid both and go for the real thing. But if you *had* to choose between the first two? John Smith's Cornflakes are defiantly, honestly different. Kelogs are obviously the work of an illiterate fraudster. Let's go for honest John. All this is to illustrate that images are precious things and the image components over which we have some power should be handled with great and continuing care.

Image governs our attitudes, relationships and behaviour towards the person or thing imagined – whether friend, a relative, colleague, car, the garden, a piece of music, or product. Whatever decision you have to make or want to make about anyone or anything, your image of that person or thing is the decisive influence. Here's proof. What was the last decision you made – other than to read this page? Was it to buy a morning paper? Ask yourself why you want a paper when the radio or television has later news, and why you bought the paper you did when most of the other titles contained the same news items. I suggest that it was your 'image' of the newspaper that determined your choice.

The power of image explains the truth of that well-known saying:

A man convinced against his will
Is of the same opinion still.

A person's will expresses that person's image of a person, product or company. If the will, governed by the image, says 'no', logical arguments in favour will cut no ice ('don't confuse me with the facts'). Likewise if it says 'yes'. This is why the brand stays king – and incidentally why the Queen of England stays on her throne. The logical arguments for making the United Kingdom a United Republic are difficult to refute in purely logical terms but are demolished when the argument centres on image. The British Royal Family is one of the world's greatest and longest-lasting brands.

In summary, persuasion based on facts can never be as powerful as persuasion based on image. Whether product or company, the brand with its image will always beat the unbranded or even the own brand, which by definition do not have images. And it will certainly beat the product or company whose pre-purchase appearances are only on the Internet. The Internet can contribute to image. It cannot create or maintain one without the help of all the other influences that affect people's attitudes and purchasing decisions. No one medium can, because 'image' is created in people's minds from an amalgam of all the influences brought to bear on them, the 'all' including advertisements and nowadays the Internet, but most especially, experience of the product. The Internet hypists claim that the brand is dead. They are talking self-evident nonsense. Are they going to stop people experiencing the product, or talking to other people about their experience of the product. Are they going to stop people looking at posters, press ads, leaflets, point of sale? Brands will live as long as there are people able to enjoy them.

I apologise for going on at this length, but we all need reminding that none of us ever makes decisions about anything on purely factual, rational, intellectual grounds, but on an amalgam of every possible fact, memory, impression, experience, all over time and all matured and fermented in the subconscious, plus the imperatives of the moment. It really is a case of 'All-to-One', with all the relevant material coming together over time to form one image in your head.

That applies to the images of products and companies no less than to the images of people and every other creature and thing.

Take product image first

It's obvious to all and deniable by none that three sets of factors combine to induce a person to buy this product or service rather than that, or to buy anything at all. One set of factors consists of what used to be called 'hard-sell' benefits. The second set used to be called 'soft-sell' benefits. The third set concerns the place where the product or service is bought.

Hard-sell benefits can be described in words and demonstrated in pictures. Some of them you can measure with a ruler. Manufacturers, traditionally, used to list these hard-sell benefits in their assumed order of importance to consumers and make sure their products had most of the most important. The more sophisticated manufacturers picked out one particular benefit and endeavoured to convince consumers (and themselves) that this benefit was really the most important, what's more their product had more of it than anybody else's did.

Other manufacturers, even more sophisticated, accepting that their and competing products were essentially identical, carried out a detailed analysis of product benefits and consumer needs/wants and ended up with a benefit common to all the products, attractive to consumers, but overlooked by other manufacturers. This benefit was also presented as a unique selling proposition, with its inevitable acronym, USP. USP led to absurdities, which were silly enough to be charming. One brewer is supposed to have given 'Our bottles are steam-washed' as a unique reason for buying his beer, when every other brewer steam-washed their bottles and who cares anyhow.

As you can guess, nit picking of this intensity got no one very far. People tend to take hard-sell benefits for granted and, as such, tend to think them boring. Mostly they are the price of admission to the market, and a contributor only to the final buying decision.

While we're talking about hard facts and benefits, it's worth highlighting the quite phenomenal growth in manufacturing efficiency – stimulated by the total quality management movement and its zero-defect rule. In addition, the ISO (Organization for International Standardization) and other official bodies are enforcing ever-higher standards across all manufacturing sectors. The company that fails to deliver its products to specification will be pilloried and in public. Everyone, not just business people, can take the hard-sell facts as read.

But if hard sell isn't enough, manufacturers can always reach into the soft-sell set and talk about those intangibles that constitute product personality. In the old days, advertising agencies were told to think of the product as a 'person', with 'human attributes'. They used words like 'caring', 'friendly', 'exciting'. The manufacturing company often featured in the publicity with its pedigree prominent and pictures of happy workers ('contented cows' as one advertiser with a milk product used to say). If you spent enough on the soft sell, and if you chose your words and pictures carefully, it could work.

Business people are still people

Just as an aside, though it's wholly relevant, let's consider for a moment the myth that tough battle-tried business consumers buy on the basis of the hard-sell benefits while other lesser folk, teenagers say, buy on the basis of the soft sell. Experience doesn't justify that antithesis. Nor does a moment's reflection. After all, business consumers are still people. They are busy and preoccupied, as is everyone else. They like to see the facts and usually study them with more insider knowledge than the average new-car buyer deploys when reading the new-car catalogue. But they haven't got the time to check whether each of the factual benefits listed is truly factual and beneficial. B2B is the most rapidly growing e-commerce sector. It provides buyers with every possible fact and figure, every one completely up to the minute. Information overload is, of course, a possibility, leading to carelessness, laziness and 'simply do what we did last time'. But even the most conscientious buyer, scanning every line on every screen, has to take things on trust – time is too short for any other response. So the final buying decision as often as not is made on trust, on gut feeling, on instinct, on an overall impression, on image, because people assume, and usually correctly assume, that the company image they prefer has all the important relevant factual benefits built into it.

What President Reagan wrote to General Powell

President Reagan, no slouch at public relations, and very much aware of his own image, was not afraid to write on a souvenir photograph of himself that he gave to his Chief of Staff, General Colin Powell, the simple phrase, 'If you say so, Colin...'. The General, of course, had earned the President's trust over the years by his achievements and because of his character, and those words of Reagan and the thought behind them encapsulate how even the most meticulous, anally-obsessive business buyer in the end makes the buying decision: 'If you say so, General Motors...', 'If you say so, Rolls Royce...', though not, of course, 'If you say so, Boo.com...'.

The third of the sets of factors governing buying decisions covers the point of sale and the means of delivery. The point of sale can be either physical or virtual, offline or online. Delivery is still very largely offline. All e-commerce, other than those few product categories that can be downloaded, is delivered offline. But off or on, the requirements are that the product or service should be properly displayed, be readily available and be in good condition. No show, no sale, certainly no casual sale, no argument about it. But this set of factors is mainly mechanical. The main exception at the point of sale is the pack design and any point-of-sale publicity. The form this takes depends on whether you choose to make the appeal mainly hard sell or soft.

So far as any consideration of image is concerned, these distinctions are irrelevant. 'Image' embraces everything, is the summation of everything. The truth is that brands (as products and as companies) succeed when *everything* about them is adjudged acceptable by the consumer. It really is 'All-to-One', the 'One' in this case being the image, the 'All' including all the advertising, all the hard-sell benefits, all the soft-sell benefits too, all aspects at the point of sale, all the news items in the media, all the people in the company making the products, and all other influences to which the consumer has been and is exposed. These other influences include the consumer's own experience of the product and what other people have to say about their experience of the product. It also includes editorial in the media. 'All' means all.

Over time, this 'all' develops into what is popularly known as the 'image' of the product, service or company. The image is slightly different to each of us because the outside influences react with the differences that are already there inside, consciously or subconsciously within our memories. A young mother's image of a baby powder will be slightly different from her own mother's image of the same powder. But because each person's image of a product is the summation of every kind of benefit, hard, soft and point of sale and every influence that person has taken on board, it is clear that the image governs all buying decisions.

That's my marmalade

People love image, whether brand image or company image. I can put that in other words. Consider your own buying habits – and when it comes to brands, 'habits' is the right word. It's annoying when you can't lay hands on your favourite marmalade (for marmalade fans a favourite brand is a very happy habit). Let's say your favourite marmalade is Cooper's Oxford. You've enjoyed it since you were – anyhow for a long time. Oxford sounds good and wasn't that where marmalade began – something like that. You know the price is OK and the fruit content is as specified and as required by some government department or other. And so on. Your image of the product is rounded and without question mark. Excuse my non-psychological language, but haven't you created a Cooper's Oxford marmalade hole in your psyche that can only be filled by that brand of marmalade? And doesn't that make your decision to buy Cooper's a kind of need, a kind of instinct? I think it does.

'Image', as developed by each of us for a particular product or service, is really 'instinct'. It is the most important attribute any supplier of products or service can own.

Cowboys?

Have you heard the Marlboro cigarette story? It's said to be true, and if it's not true historically, it's true where it counts – in the moral it imparts. The owner of the Marlboro brand was allegedly asked – by an admiring competitor – if his company was for sale. Certainly, came the reply, let's talk price. To arrive at a fair valuation, they went through the company's assets one by one: factories? Price soon agreed. Delivery vans and the like? No problem over price. Sales force? The would-be buyer simply undertook to keep them all on at the same salaries. Finally the discussion came round to the name 'Marlboro', its associated image of the cowboy (cleverly poised between that of a real cowboy and of a rich man on his ranch), and the right to use it. How much for all that? No deal, was the reply, Take everything except that. I can build any number of new factories, hire more sales reps, drivers, trucks and warehouses. I can't rebuild the Marlboro name and the image surrounding it.

OK so you don't smoke, and yes, the BBC did run a series showing that one particular Marlboro cowboy model did indeed have lung cancer. But the image was wonderfully powerful (Leo Burnett, head of the agency of that ilk, described the Marlboro cowboy pictures as the work of 'open-pore photography' – you couldn't fault Leo on presentation) and in its heyday was worth untold billions of dollars to its owner, Philip Morris.

You're forgiven, Leo

But 'image' is not only a bankable asset, bankable that is if you are prepared to sell and bankable in the money it generates for you. It also works for good in another vital way. It strengthens your forgivability.

This is what happens. There is a blemish in one of your products/ services or in your consumer communications. It happens from time to time in the best companies. Consumers have two main choices: they can blame you, and maybe withdraw their custom temporarily – perhaps permanently if the blemish is perceived as serious; or they can forgive you.

Now if, over the years, you have successfully presented your company as a caring, thoughtful, and competent organisation, and proved it by your products and general behaviour, if that is your image, then the consumer is likely to assume that the blemish is untypical, and rank bad luck, and that for certain you'll be putting it right and it won't happen again in a hurry, or else it stems from something completely outside your control, or else it's just part of the human condition. After all, the Marlboro brand is still riding high in spite of the cancer scare.

The psychological basis for this apparently contradictory behaviour is that human beings shrink from the condition known as 'cognitive dissonance', defined as an uncomfortable state resulting from conflicting perceptions of an object. To avoid such dissonance, people subconsciously adapt any new perceptions that are dissonant with their existing perceptions in order to make them consonant. The reaction to the mistake then becomes: 'it's so unlike this company to make a mistake like that. Perhaps it's not really their fault ... perhaps it's not really a mistake ... in any event, whatever it is, I'm sure it's all for the best and they'll soon put it right.'

Mr Gladstone's top hat

The classic non-commercial example usually given concerns Mr William Ewart Gladstone, the great and exceedingly correct Victorian Prime Minister and his top hat, which, of course, was always removed in the presence of a lady. On one never-to-be-forgotten occasion, he is alleged to have entered Queen Victoria's presence wearing his top hat, which he then failed to remove. The Queen and her courtiers made no comment. Why not? Because whatever else they thought of him, their relevant perception was of Mr Gladstone as an extremely well-mannered gentleman (the Queen

in fact couldn't stand him and thought him more than a little mad).
If he continued to wear his top hat when normal etiquette required
its removal it was either because: (a) he had a bad head cold; or (b) he
had just had a slight but unpleasant-looking head injury and wished
to spare the Queen the sight of blood; or (c) he was temporarily mad,
which he couldn't help, and anyhow that nice Mr Disraeli would
soon be back in office. Whatever, the refusal was not caused by
discourtesy.

Mr Gladstone's gentlemanly, courteous image in the minds of
courtiers and others was not won overnight. Just like a product or
company image, it was put together over many years, in many
different circumstances and in many different 'media'. In WEG's case
the 'media' would have been Eton, Oxford, the House of Commons,
the Privy Council, his books and speeches, his table talk, his family,
his chopping down of trees (his main outdoor hobby) and such like.

As I said earlier, 'image' only exists in the mind, obviously so
because it is the mind's own creation. It is what the mind has created
over time from the amalgam of all the many different kinds of
influence, exposure and experience. Above all, it is the result of a
totality of exposure to the product (or company), not just its
projection in the media, not just its parade of hard-sell and soft-sell
benefits, not just its attractive availability at the point of sale, not
just its appearance in the editorial parts of the media, but more, the
more being the person's own experiences of the product and the
experiences and opinions of friends, family and acquaintances as
related to that person. All these are the 'All' in 'All-to-One'.

The nub of my position vis-à-vis the 'one-to-one' concept is that
by its very nature it cannot create, sustain or even deliver the full
range of influences needed to create or help create a worthwhile
'image' in the minds of consumers and prospects. The depth,
breadth and roundness that characterise a successful 'image' are
utterly beyond it. It is therefore fatally flawed as a selling tool.

The next step in this argument stands out a mile.

'All-to-One' is uniquely able to help create, sustain, develop and
project the 'image' of a product or a company – because 'All-to-One'
delivers everything the mind needs to create that image.

Commercial transactions are public property

There's a further point, and it really is of the greatest importance. The great and fundamental mistake the Internet enthusiasts make is to imagine that commercial transactions in our world are between two sets of people – buyers and sellers – and that these transactions can be carried out, as between consenting adults, in the privacy of the Internet without any outside interference ever and without any downside.

Absolutely, devastatingly wrong at every level.

At the level of the marketplace, the social level, the mistake is to assume that it is always and only the person who does the actual buying who is involved in the buying decision. Wrong. People prefer to make buying decisions in an aura of approval, before, during and after purchase (there will always be exceptions, most of them in their middle teens).

Don't forget the neighbours

Take a young couple setting up home. They tend to make joint decisions to buy, even if only one of them actually does the buying. Pardon my male chauvinism, if that's what it is, but assume that in this instance it's the woman who does the buying and wants the man's approval for her choice of brand. If the Internet is her only source of information, does she invite him to join her at the screen or to log on himself? Likely? Not really. A far more likely scenario is that he saw the thing advertised on TV or somewhere and noticed it as well on a sticker in a shop window, or knew the name of the brand from years back and said what a good idea darling. And what does mother think? And mother-in-law? And the neighbours? None of them will have learnt what to think from the relevant site on the Internet because none of them is likely to have accessed it. Why should they? The fact is that people pick up ideas about products from a very wide range of sources, most of all from sources such as TV commercials, street posters and shop window displays which they did not deliberately access.

Or, take a man buying a lawn mower. Does he care what his wife thinks? Only to the extent that if she doesn't approve, he'll never hear the last of it. So he buys a named make that she's heard of, one that sounds good to her, one whose nice picture appeared in one of last Sunday's supplements. A secretive deal on the Internet with a company that only exists electronically is not conducive to married harmony. (By the way, I notice that at the time of writing Amazon, the Internet-based bookseller, has adopted the slogan 'A *real* company in a virtual world' – which is at least lip-service to the point I'm making.)

There's also the fact that the person buying the product is not the user of it, or not the only user. The classic example is shopping for food. Nearly always, the buyer is buying for someone else as well. All the users and not just the buyer have to be convinced that the product is right. 'I bought it through the Internet' is not an automatic seal of approval. There has to be outside endorsement, which the Internet can't give.

Brands still best

At the level of individual preference, the Internet-only approach is still inadequate. People like *brands*, they like to be seen using brands that their friends and relations admire or at least accept. They are proud to wear a Rolex; glad to be seen driving a Volvo; confident about Mum; happy to pass round the After-Eights and so on *ad paradisum*. A product or company accessed only through the Internet is not likely to gain that kind of brand status. The reason is that brands really are quite like people. You get to know people when you see them against different backgrounds in different ambiences. The person you meet only through teleconferencing is a stranger compared with the person you actually work with in the same office, and you don't know that person as well as you know your neighbour with whom you also play tennis and meet in the local newsagent. Brands like people get real when they are seen and learnt about in many different ways in many different media.

So, at both those levels, the social and the individual, the

Internet-only company/brand will lose consumers. That's bad enough. But at the highest level of all, it could lose its very right to exist. It could be forced out of business.

Secrecy has no future

The reason is simple. We are a free society. Openness is our strength. At the highest level, the secrecy of the Internet constitutes a potential threat to our free society, a threat our free society simply will not tolerate. The threat needs careful explanation. No one wants to or could interfere with people's right to trade on the Internet in private. But the companies and people doing so should realise the inherent and unavoidable risk they are taking.

It centres round the concept of a company's 'right to operate'. The concept came to the fore in this country at the time of Shell UK's Brent Spar fiasco five years ago, when in spite of every intelligent and responsible step taken by the company, it was accused of riding rough-shod over the people, the environment and every assumed international agreement. The incident sprang from Shell's sensible (as it thought) decision to sink its Brent Spar floating oil storage tank, the only one of its kind in the world, but then past its use-by date, in the North Atlantic. Other disposal options seemed to be more environmentally unfriendly. However, the green lobbyists got to work, their unsoundly based accusations stuck, some Shell service stations in Europe were firebombed and boycotts began to bite. Shell was concerned, to put it mildly. It had tried so hard, it had been a better citizen for longer than most, and still its honour was being impugned. The deeper risk, as Shell knew only too well, was that its 'licence to operate' might be withdrawn.

'Licence to operate'

What is this 'licence to operate'? It is an informal, unspoken, unofficial but indispensable agreement between a company and society. In return for what society perceives to be good behaviour, the company is allowed to continue. If society approves, nothing untoward happens and the company can get on with its business. If society disapproves, still nothing untoward appears to happen, there's usually no great ceremony with muffled drums, muskets held upside down and insignia of rank torn off – though I suppose something like that could happen if and when Microsoft gets a come-uppance from the US government. No, unless government is involved, or the media decide to have a public lynching (when the end comes very quickly), all that usually happens is a quiet 'not-today-thank-you' from millions of people. That's all. It's a death sentence. Ask Gerald Ratner, once eponymous head of Ratners, the once great high-street jewellery chain, ask the heads of the dozens of companies, on and off the Internet, who every year pay the ultimate price for getting it wrong with society.

Now, the e-commerce companies make things so much worse for themselves. Society has no way of telling whether a company whose outward manifestations appear only on screen is behaving itself or not. Society has better things to do with its time than follow the activities of each and every one of the millions of companies selling things through the screen. But equally, when things go wrong and the e-commerce company is hauled before the courts or the tabloids for some misdemeanour, society has no opinion about the company – how could it? – and the company has to stay sunk in the mess it has created for itself. Shell, on the other hand, had spent billions over the years in every kind of media telling society what it did, what it sold and what its aims were. No one with eyes and ears and who walked around in the daylight could fail to know about Shell.

Result: in spite of accusations of the gravest kind (although in this case somewhat unjustified), Shell was allowed to continue, the bombing and boycotts stopped and the company's reputation is now back as high as ever – some would say higher because it also had the grace to apologise.

At the heart of all this is the aforementioned 'forgivability' and you cannot expect society to be forgiving if it knows nothing about the company that needs forgiveness. It happens that the Internet can't communicate with society because the Internet is a one-to-one, person-to-person medium, isn't it?

Therefore, successful companies who want to go on being successful know that their true target market extends far beyond the individuals sitting at home, faces fixed on their screen with the mouse at the ready and the credit card to hand. It includes people it may never sell anything to at all — the friends, relations and neighbours of the actual consumer. But pre-eminently, it also includes society as a whole. Society is the most important, the most influential and the most powerful market of all. It must be kept on side. The Internet can't help with that requirement.

The nub of it all is that image is the motivator for everything everybody does, thinks or feels. Image is in charge. And so far as companies, services and products are concerned, if they are successful as brands, it is because their image is right.

Image rules to make brand the king.

No rewards without risk

'All-to-One' requires openness from everyone in the company, it also requires everyone in the company to respond positively to consumer calls. What if the call is a complaint? Excellent. There's ample research evidence, as well as common sense, to say that every time a consumer is the victim at the receiving end of a mistake by a company, he or she will discuss the mistake with anyone who will listen – as many as a dozen, perhaps more. But what happens if the company puts that mistake right, handsomely? The victim suddenly becomes a hero, someone who has brought out the best in a company and demonstrated the value of an individual to that company. How many people are then told about the success? Far more than heard the original complaint. So natural and predictable is this human reaction that some companies actually advertise for people to make complaints. The word-of-mouth publicity they get from putting those mistakes right more than justifies the costs involved.

Who manages the consumer relationship best?

Q UICK ANSWER: those who can take the 'All-to-One' approach. Over the years the car manufacturers and their franchised dealers have been at loggerheads about the relationship each has or should have with the consumer. The manufacturer is in ultimate control of the brand, the specification, the price, the marketing and promotion, the PR, the everything – except direct interactive contact with consumers. That is the prerogative of the dealers. So neither side can offer 'All-to-One' service because the 'All' is divided in two. There are further complications. The dealership selling the car is not always the one servicing it.

Change is on the way. The Internet promises to give consumers the chance to bypass the unsatisfactory dealer and go to the manufacturer for information – but go back to the dealer for actual servicing. In other words, the Internet implements the full 'All-to-One' approach by effectively connecting the selling and servicing, the manufacturer and the dealer, and so give the consumer the benefit of everyone's attention.

This is how it could work – indeed is starting to work now. Buyers of new and used cars can make their initial short-list of models via the Internet, book a test drive in the same way and have the test-drive car turn up at their home by appointment.

Specifications and price can be agreed on the Internet, and any required finance can also be arranged there.

Servicing and repairs can be carried by online arrangements. The consumer's car is collected from a designated pick-up point and serviced in a facility shared with other brands using the same facilities. Then delivered back to the consumer – who has no interest in where the car is serviced as long as the quality of work matches that laid down by the manufacturer. At the present rate of technology development, it will soon be possible to 'remote-service' the car while it is stationary outside the consumer's home, or even while being driven down a motorway. The dominant role of the dealers as the 'gate-keepers' will go (unless their service radically improves), leaving their premises as shop-windows for the window-shoppers, who will reserve their serious buying decisions to interactivity with the manufacturer on the Internet. Meantime, the manufacturers' advertising and promotions chime in with the messages given through the Internet and 'All-to-One' is within reach.

So with these apocalyptic thoughts in mind, ask yourself what the dealers are doing now to make their still dominant but threatened role more secure. Here are some facts:

Out of all test drives that are generated through a dealer only 25 per cent convert to a sale. Reasons for the low conversion rate range from dissatisfaction with product and its specifications to dissatisfaction with dealers and their location (this issue will become less contentious as car collection and delivery services start to be provided by the manufacturers working in close collaboration with their dealers or at least that had better happen before new entrants – such as Virgin cars with its 'home service' – force their hand).

On average most dealers at point of sale fail to close the sale, with poor consumer management leading often to overall prospect dissatisfaction. Further, even when a test drive has been completed, the dealer seems reluctant to follow up the prospect if an automatic sale does not occur.

What follows is more subjective, though it represents my own feelings as a new-car prospect.

I recently conducted a personal mystery shop of my own, visiting 11 franchised dealerships. Out of all of those, only one actually called back to enquire whether I was still interested in buying the car I had test driven. Of the remaining 10, one eventually called to offer me an extended test drive but only because he had been given my name by the manufacturer's call centre following an enquiry I had made previously for a product brochure and price list.

Remember: this is a one-man mystery shop, but I report as I found and I was genuinely in the market for a car.

The worst of those I visited was the Mercedes Benz dealership. In my opinion, as I thought at the time and think so now, they were arrogant, unprofessional, uncaring, everything was too much trouble. Perhaps I was unlucky. Perhaps it was something I said! But here's a tip: if your nearest Mercedes Benz dealer is anything like the one I visited, never tell them you are interested in a used car. You are instantly relegated to the bottom division.

The second worst was the Audi – I tell you how it struck me at the time, other people might report differently. There was no follow up. When I remarked on this, I got the classic reply 'Well Sir, there was no point – you can't get the model you are after for 9 months!'

VW, from the same mould as Audi, seemed to me to share a similar ordering malaise.

Rover appeared to have trouble dealing with any genuine enquiry at all, but at the time they were overshadowed by their big brother BMW.

The best premium brand dealerships I visited were Volvo and Saab, although I know that both have major problems in closing a sale.

The volume car dealerships I visited varied, in my opinion, from the good (Ford and Vauxhall) to the not so good (Peugeot) to the even less good (Daewoo). Sorry chaps, I'm merely saying what I thought at the time of my visit.

So what happened next?

There is a courtship period in the car-buying cycle. Whatever format it takes, it doesn't come cheap. So you'd think the dealers would get together with the manufacturers to get their act together and clinch the deal.

Witness one such case: some many months ago Volvo had a stately home drive-day for their new s80, a superb location for a superb car. The day cost Volvo and presumably the dealership about £150 per prospect per head so you think they would be keen to sell the car!

I was invited, went and was impressed by the car. But there was no follow up by anybody. Four months later, there was still no follow up, not even a phone call to ask whether I was still in the market for a car!

Eventually I bought a car by telephone. That's what happened next! I knew the car and its specification – so there was no real need for a test drive. All finance and insurance was handled on the telephone. All I had to do was pick up the car from the dealership.

And that's where the problems started again.

Never take delivery of a car late in the evening 30 minutes away from the dealership closing time and on the night England play in a major championship. Everybody is too preoccupied to bother with you. That was the night I chose.

Two weeks later, I have had not one telephone call from either the manufacturer or dealer asking whether I was happy with the car or the service, and about my overall satisfaction with both the product and the dealership.

So there is already a feeling running through my mind whether I should take my car for servicing to the selling dealer or find another one closer to home.

This one-man's bad experience is, I believe, an accurate reflection of an overall malaise: the short-term approach which dealers adopt to selling and to consumer relationship marketing generally. It is common throughout the industry and offers no answer to the threat of the coming new technology whereby consumers will be able to carry out all their purchasing and servicing transactions online without dealer intervention.

The dealers fight the manufacturers, blinded by their fear that the manufacturers may want to go direct – but it is not in their interests to do so. The manufacturers' interest is in the dealers giving consumers better service, selling more cars and keeping aftersales consumers for longer. The Internet, linked to call centres through mobile and WAP telephony technology and with an interactive database, will give someone the wherewithal to conduct mutually profitable long-term relationships with consumers.

Whether the manufacturers or the dealers do it depends on action each side takes now.

But the biggest threat could be a new entrant to the game from the financial services world, or from the retail world (Tesco already sells vehicles, well scooters, direct to its consumers with a home service, insurance package, training course and so forth) or the Autobytels of this world.

My guess is that the manufacturers will come out on top because only they can provide the 'All-to-One' experience. The dealers will always be handicapped because so many of the factors that make for purchase fall beyond their conceivable remit – the product itself for a start. But the manufacturers have a lot to achieve in a short space of time. Online transactions and transaction analysis will be better enabled through the new technology, but the challenge will be to achieve a seamless interface with prospects and consumers in which all the points of contact between company and consumer are unified. Given the performance of current call centre managed brands, the call centres will need a complete overhaul.

That reminds me. The call centre still hasn't phoned to confirm my first service visit.

Mini case study

Recruiting students at a Christian college in Indiana

IN COMPARISON WITH my car-buying experience, my friend, Derek Kaufman who runs a wonderfully successful IT consulting business on the West Coast, tells me about his eldest son and his choice of university. He had a wide choice, the field was open. One of the possibilities was Taylor University in Upland Indiana. This is a small private Christian college with a very wired-up way of recruiting new students. After Derek's boy had visited the place for a preliminary look-see, he got a series of calls from students already in residence. A young lady called him one night to ask how his High School soccer team was doing. Every week he got a mailing about some facet or other of college life. He was the 'One' and he was wooed by the 'All' of the college. What happened next? At the time of writing, decisions are still being made.

I guess the decision will be: 'This Taylor suits me'.

Nine

Creating an 'All-to-One' culture in your company

Six years ago, a high-tech company created a small subsidiary of a larger company, because a small group of its people wanted to pursue a few good ideas. The 'small' subsidiary now has over 7,000 people. It says that its culture is all about people and creativity. However, it dislikes standardisation – so much that it frequently misses sales opportunities because no one can agree on the response they should make.

An Internet provider has set up an automated response system for 'complaint' e-mails received. If you e-mail a complaint, you get a reply by return suggesting that you look at their help section on the website (implication: you're an idiot who hasn't read the instructions!). If you still want to complain, you have to send another e-mail. And when they reply – albeit within 12 hours – their reply is titled 'Resolution of your complaint no. 123'. Interesting when the complaint hasn't been resolved.

A train company unexpectedly closes both its sales desks at 7.30 am one Wednesday morning. So you can't buy a ticket, but you know you'll be fined for travelling without one. The only automatic ticket machine on the station is out of order. There are no officials around to tell you why the sales desks were closed, but you find out from another traveller who learnt from somebody else that there had been a small fire in the station office! You know you'll be late for your meeting!

A check-in agent in the airport at Eindhoven replies to your complaint about a problem with your ticket by saying, 'Well, it's nothing to do with me. They make the decisions. (Remember, she's an agent, not a member of the airline's staff.) She says that she's never seen this type of ticket before, but you know that it has been heavily promoted by the airline for over a year. You've been up since 4.30 that morning and begin to wonder why you bother being a member of their frequent flyer loyalty scheme. You're due to fly to Zurich the following week. You decide to fly with another airline.

The new general manager of a private hospital announces his arrival with a piece in the hospital newsletter, complete with picture. Six weeks after his arrival, he has still not been seen by any of the nurses on the wards. He then turns up at a ward reception desk with his family saying that he wants to show them what a typical ward looks like. He doesn't give his name, assuming that the receptionist knows who he is.

EACH OF THESE five horror stories, anonymised to protect the guilty, is based on real-life incidents involving me or one or other of my clients. You could probably think of several similar. All the stories show how the culture of an enterprise can affect for good or bad its relationship with consumers and the relationship between members of its staff. All the organisations involved probably have marketing strategies. All of them will have had meetings recently when they all agreed that relationships with consumers and between members of staff are very important. Some of them might be investing a mountain of money in CRM or other ways of planning and managing to get closer to their consumers. But none of this effort matters to the consumers – or to the staff for that matter if the results are not good. All they are concerned with is how it affects them. If it affects them badly, no amount of money, meetings and effort will cut any ice with them. It certainly didn't with me and my clients.

It comes back to the 'All-to-One' approach creating an 'All-to-One' culture. Unless everyone and everything in the enterprise, the *extended* enterprise, is properly consumer-oriented, then 'All-to-One' cannot work as it should. In the long run, it is all or nothing.

'All-to-One' is not a bolt-on extra. It has to pervade the whole, extended enterprise. It has to be implicit in everything the enterprise thinks, feels and does. 'Culture' is a convenient word to describe all that and a company without an 'All-to-One' culture cannot hope to implement an 'All-to-One' business philosophy. How could it? It would be a contradiction in terms. The 'All' in 'All-to-One' must include all people in the company, all its systems, traditions, attitudes and actions. What that means in practice is explained here.

Companies have cultures whether they like it or not, whether they know it or not. It's a fact of life. Cultures develop whenever people live or work together over any length of time. Left to themselves, they'll develop in their own sweet inward-looking way and usually end on a sour note with the company bust and the employees out of a job. A self-generated and self-perpetuating culture of this kind is not much more than 'how we do things round here'. Human beings being what they are, the way we do things is usually the one that causes the least trouble and gives us all an easy, cosy life. Nothing wrong with that if you're living on inherited capital – as many companies in fact are. If you're aiming to grow the company into something more worth while, something you can be proud of, you need to do something. But what? The answer to that is easy: 'look outwards, look at the consumer'. That is the direction from which growth and sustainability always come.

When the group is a company fighting for its place in today's sun, then the outward look must always be towards the consumer. Today, the consumer is more than the centre of your business. The consumer is your business. Any company whose culture makes the well-being of staff, or their careers, or the standing of the chief executive (yes, it's been known to happen) or even the value of the stock the first priority has nemesis in store. Staff well-being and their future careers, most certainly the price of the stock and even the CEO's standing at the country club depend utterly on the consumer. The culture must be wholly and continually consumer-facing. If the consumer says no, everyone else and everything else supply the echo.

However, just as with the marketing we have to start from where we are now – and RelModel shows how – so with the culture. The right culture cannot be created overnight. But believe this: without the right complementary and supportive culture, every effort made to attain, one after the other, the RelModel targets will have failure branded right through them. 'All-to-One', the guiding principle of the RelModel, must apply in full colour to the company culture whatever stage it might be at. Above all, there must be the same connectivity with the consumer as there is with the marketing. The culture and the marketing are completely intertwined and interdependent.

As on the marketing side, the RelModel methodology allows you to identify the stage your company is at, and join in at the right level before proceeding upwards. So you can with the culture.

In a way, the RelModel applied to the creation or development of a company culture is simpler. At least it looks simpler. But because the 'raw material' of culture is people, who come already equipped with their own culture, that is their own set of attitudes, ambitions, foibles and prejudices, the task of shaping it in real life is subtle and requires time. There's no quick fix. But if people can be persuaded of the need for a culture – and you may not ever use the word – then creating and implementing one becomes more straightforward.

All this is to say that the culture should be an all-company endeavour, one that must be backed by the boss and the board who should be among the most prominent exponents of it.

The 'All-to-One' approach has many advantages – it provides a methodology for one thing. But the key advantage is that its emphasis is outward-looking, always on to the consumer. This is far from being a difficult concept for anyone to understand. It comes naturally to human nature, as naturally as does its reverse. But given a choice and the right encouragement, most people prefer to look outwards rather than inwards. The 'All-to-One' culture goes with the grain.

It's important to emphasise that the sequence of events outlined below can only give 'signposts' pointing in the direction you should be going. I have added, after the sequence, some rather more detailed points about the whole subject.

Level 1

The culture is fragmented and inward looking. Departments and even groups within departments are concerned with protecting their own patch. Loyalty to these various subcultures is strong but there is no joint outlook, no joint aims, no vision for the whole company. Internal politics get you promoted – or the reverse. There is not a consumer focus initiative in sight. Fear of getting things wrong pervades. Risk is discouraged. Wise words about people-care are greeted with suspicion and scepticism.

Level 2

A company at Level 2 has the beginnings of an outward-looking culture, but the culture itself is still fragmented, with separate departments still operating their own codes of practice and attitude. However, in some departments, most likely the sales and marketing departments, the culture starts to look outside at the consumer and how best the consumer can be served.

Level 3

The company is now overall far more consumer-driven, and so as a result are all the departments within it. Although people are now starting to realise that the consumer is the only reason for existence in their job, there is a still a powerful tendency towards department loyalty, and how the department can help their internal consumers, the sales and marketing people, to do their job. The prospects for the development of an optimum working culture look good, with people working smoothly across the old departmental borders.

Level 4

Everyone in the company now has a clearer view of the consumers and potential consumers 'out there' and recognises that consumers only remain consumers (and consumers become your consumers) if they receive the products they want or need and of a better quality and more caring service than they expected. People realise that satisfying each consumer's needs is the responsibility of everyone in the company.

Level 5

Everyone in the company now realises that the aim is to convert consumers into loyal friends-for-life. The 'All-to-One' concept is now being fulfilled. The 'All' now includes, as it must, all the people in the company. What's more, each and every person has to be convinced of their vital role as part of that whole. There is a recognition for a need to drive continually towards the satisfaction of consumer needs and that constant effort to keep ahead of consumers is the only way to remain at this level.

Technology needs people

Increasingly technology is playing a very important part in the day-to-day operations of commerce. 'All-to-One' makes full use of it, but as you move up the levels of RelModel, service delivery becomes an integral part of successful implementation. People therefore play a crucial part in that implementation, and therefore culture plays a key role.

Paradoxically, increased technology puts greater weight on the company's people and their culture because it raises consumer expectations. They now expect to be treated as individuals at all times, and not just on those occasions when the technology can operate on its own. So it's important that the required cultures reach all the corporate corners, even those outside the company but acting on its behalf such as travel agents for the airlines and car dealers for the motor manufacturers, the so-called extended enterprise.

Staying in business over a period of time requires that the business keeps in tune with the market and ahead of the competition. The market dictates, and service is often a key differentiator. Computers can spot trends and be used to highlight problems but it is people on the ground who will pick up problems first or prevent them becoming problems in the first place. Those on the ground can also look more intelligently at information and, given the scope, can work creatively to prevent problems escalating. Good service is as much about dealing well with exceptions as good underlying standards, which are increasingly required as a minimum to do business with the public.

The new 'All-to-One' culture therefore requires:

1. that the importance and context of service is understood

2. that the important role of people is acknowledged and understood

3. that the rate of change is acknowledged

4. that those involved are helped to cope with the pressures of change

5. that the culture is set in place to embrace and use the benefits of change

6. that taking risk and acting by exception is encouraged and rewarded

7. that all the elements of service delivery are brought into the equation so there is no hot and cold experience for the consumer

8. that the increasing demands and knowledge of consumers are factored into planning and investment.

Companies now have to deal with a number of conflicting strands: reducing cost of sale; coping with accelerating change; massive changes brought about by technology and most of all an intelligent and demanding consumer base that has far greater access to tools of comparison and alternatives. However, the full benefits of keeping

Changing cultures in a changing world

A culture that works for a company must be based on 'joint aims, joint values'. 'All-to-One' reminds us that the aims and values must be totally consumer-oriented – which means they must take fully into account not only the consumer's personal aspirations but also the consumer's view of the community and the world. They must also take into account the view held by members of the staff. To give a simple example – a company culture that seemed to be uncaring about the effect the company's products had on young people would not work. It would command no one's assent.

It is easily arguable that today the two main outside issues on which the vast majority of employees (and consumers too) have strong views are the environment and the Third World. Some people still don't care about such 'liberal' issues, or at best think they have nothing to do with the business world they inhabit, but most consumers and most staff do care. Even more to the point, the kind of people who can gain a company promotion to the premier division in its chosen business sphere, and then to the top, do care and they tend not to tolerate company targets that hit the environment adversely or have a negative effect on Third-World poverty. This ethical dimension is comparatively new. Thirty years ago the Cold War was the dominant world problem, with 'environment' simply a posh word for office decor and the 'Third World' some curious entity that lay way below the horizon – the name itself was only coined in the 1970s. Today, no company mission or vision statement can afford to be anti either of those concerns, even by implication. As with the mission and vision, so with the culture. The 'All-to-One' ideal cannot even be approached if the culture of the company does not square with the culture of the staff and the consumers.

consumers (loyalty) are often not taken into account and decisions on overhead and investment in good service delivery calculated on a short-term basis.

Furthermore standards go up all the time – as fast as you have established a better level as the standard so it becomes a given and rising above the rest requires even better delivery.

Good service requires a combination of training, energy and understanding of how the components fit into the whole and on certain occasions a willingness to take a risk. The rewards can be significant. There's a good, shall I say charming, example of risk taking bringing rewards. It happened that British Airways, taking a consumer from London to Brussels took his baggage to Benbecula in the Outer Hebrides by mistake. What did some enterprising risk-taking, thoroughly motivated and culture-primed British Airways employee do? He chartered a plane, that's what he did, and had the missing luggage delivered to the consumer – as it happens a Premier Club high-value consumer – who was about to give a lecture at an important European Union conference before an audience of very VIPs. His presentation was in one of the bags. He devoted the first five minutes of his lecture to a eulogy on the caring service provided by BA. To reach such a massively influential audience with a five-minute commercial, all the better because delivered by an extremely satisfied consumer, would have cost many thousands at TV commercial rates and certainly far more than the purely incremental costs of using the special aircraft. Mind you, that all happened years ago when the BA culture was in full fig.

For a business to continue to remain successful, it must have its entire staff behind it – that is the 'All-to-One' message again. This means that the staff must

❏ Understand where the company is going and support its ideals.

❏ Be given the tools to do the job – this includes training for current as well as future requirements.

❏ Recognise and embrace change.

❏ Understand that everything depends on providing consumers with what they want and staying in tune with the market.

❏ Feel that their role in good delivery is recognised and well rewarded.

❏ Look out for the unexpected and take risks where it is appropriate (as did the Benbecula hero).

❏ Acknowledge the increasing complexity of the market and plan and take advantage of it.

❏ Where necessary prioritise and target those consumers who are most valuable and have been loyal – but make sure that they take as broad a view as possible of what constitutes value (N.B. change in lifestyle stages, overall disposition, past loyalty of the consumer, etc.).

❏ Make sure that everyone in the company from the CEO to the youngest entrant wears their consumer-first credentials on their sleeves.

Developing the 'All-to-One' culture requires a great deal of investment. Above all it requires constant reinforcement of these ideals through every means possible, including:

❏ *Internal and external communication* – everyone must know 'what's going on'. The aim is to beat the grapevine.

❏ *Rewards* – the basic pay must be good and in line with performance, and so should one-off payments and special rewards for special achievements. Fat cats, for instance, do not normally encourage staff or consumer loyalty unless they are universally seen to be doing a really good job.

❏ *Training* – listening and adopting/acknowledging good ideas from everyone –especially front-line staff.

❏ *Investing in service* – in technology, staff and working conditions. Low overheads do not always produce the best business results.

❏ *Taking a medium and longer term view* – you are looking for a lifetime of value from each consumer. You should always take a holistic view of the consumer experience and ensure that all parts of the jigsaw are included.

So far we've been talking in general terms and describing 'culture' in broad brush strokes. Let's look now at the detail because it's in the detail that cultures come to life and start delivering. The practicalities need taking one by one. You have a long hit list: You need to:

❏ grow an environment in which creativity and energy interact and flourish

❏ develop a pro-active, 'doing' bias and a consumer focus/service mentality

❏ create emotional capital

❏ develop cross-functionality

❏ improve web and marketing competencies

❏ ensure that leadership is clear and visible ...

❏ ... and is supporting the corporate pyramid (the best corporations are inverted pyramids with the CEO taking the weight)

❏ stimulate a decision-making environment for everyone

❏ encourage a no-risk/no-reward mentality and accept its price (which is failure)

❏ reward skunk-hunters ('something smells wrong here')

❏ praise honesty and openness

The development of the post-Internet economy – the economy that takes the Internet for granted – is challenging most of the business paradigms we hold. 'Paradigm shift' is a phrase tripping off many people's tongues with varying degrees of exasperation or delight, depending on which side of the '30-years-old' hill they happen to be. Certainly those managers and consultants who learned their trade in the old economy, a game with different rules, have reason to be exasperated. The speed with which anyone can now do business, the instant openness of the global marketplace, the seeming in-your-face availability of everything, the ever-heightening expectations, enthusiasms and scepticisms of consumers, the merry-go-round mobility of staff and, of course, all that rocketing technology – business was never like this before. The company culture has to bring order and direction to this maelstrom so as to harness all the company's various potentials. Nothing and no one must be left out. Everyone must be 'No. 1'. 'All-to-One' provides the necessary new paradigm.

But what does that mean in practice? How do we lead and manage the people who will make 'All-to-One' a reality on a wet Monday morning? Every Monday morning, with consumers and colleagues perhaps not in the best of tempers.

And how do we get our people not just to do the right things, but to do them in the right way? Every wet Monday morning. Technology and the marketplace and the ideas that govern business organisation might change. Human beings remain the same. And when all the chips are down and the last genuflections made to the mission, the vision and the strategic plan, company culture is about how human beings actually work with other human beings.

Back to basics really. All roads in marketing lead to people.

So how do we set about creating the right culture? The good news is that it is simple. The bad news is that it is hard work. The big news is that it is about how we evolve an organisation's culture, as opposed to changing it to a set ideal.

Let's have another definition of corporate culture (another way of saying 'company culture'), this time from a highly respected marketing academic, Edgar Schein whose book, *Organisational Culture and Leadership*, published as long ago as 1985, provided a much-needed kick in the pants to previous thinking on the subject. Schein defines corporate culture as:

> '... the pattern of basic assumptions that a given group has invented, discovered or developed in learning to cope with its problems of external adaptation and internal integration and

that have worked well enough to be considered valid, and therefore to be taught to new members as the correct way to perceive, think and feel in relation to these problems.'

Or, as they say: 'the way we do things round here'.

Any organisation's culture is a function of its own personal history and development. Parts of the culture will spring from so far back in the past that people can't even remember *why* they do it this way – 'we just do'. Some of the culture will have stemmed from the values of the founders or the parent of the organisation. All companies in the Virgin group carry the stamp of the eponymous founder. You could almost believe that Richard does everything himself – sell the insurance as he was portrayed doing in the TV commercial, recommend the mortgage, serve the soft drinks, fly the aircraft, or at least the balloon, etc. There is a famous preacher, John Stott, at a famous London church, All Souls, Langham Place, near the BBC, whose sermons draw hundreds, if not thousands, so powerful is his message. His personality is imprinted on the church and on his clergymen and clergywomen colleagues who serve there. People have been known to come away from All Souls heartily inspired by a John Stott sermon when the man himself was thousands of miles away on a preaching tour in a different part of the world. Richard Branson is like that, and so is every other charismatic company founder, people of the calibre of Henry Ford, Gordon Selfridge, Mr Fortnum and Mr Mason, Charles Forte … to name but a few out of thousands. Those are the big names, but every country, every city, every village can claim a company whose culture is a reflection of the person who founded it.

Other cultures will spring not from a charismatic but from reactions to either good or bad experiences in the past. The culture of Shell was decisively changed by the 'bad' experience of the Brent Spar episode. The culture of Ford was changed with the successful launch of the Mustang back in the 1960s – the Mustang being the kind of sporty car that Ford 'just didn't make'. The culture of Marks & Spencer had better be radically changed if the department store chain is to recover its former commercial glory.

Some cultures have evolved because of conscious attempts to do things differently. Mary Quant did things differently from her competitors and succeeded. So did Daewoo cars when they first came into the UK, and they succeeded for a time. The Saturn culture of General Motors has worked. The dotcom banks are doing things differently in a big way. Talk to people working for any of those companies and you will hear and see the difference. The culture of 'difference' is a good one to take on board, particularly if you are young and have yet to make your mark.

Some cultures are modified by 'cultural viruses' brought in by new employees. The young turks brought into British Airways by Colin Marshall turned the fading gentlemen's club culture of the old BA into something that even Richard Branson would recognise.

In all this discourse, we must be careful not to imply that cultures are necessarily monocoque, sometimes they are clinker built – if you'll pardon the boating analogies. What I mean is that some corporate cultures, perhaps most, come complete in one piece and wherever you go in the company, there is the culture, a seamless overarching whole, and nothing else. But sometimes there is a series of subcultures, each self-contained, each owing something to the main culture and each contributing to it layer on layer (as with a clinker-built boat). Many professional groups within the company have their own values about how they work. Compare for instance the possible culture differences between your audit department and your field sales team! Subcultures can also be the continuing result of acquisitions or mergers between different organisational cultures. These can turn awkward and generally need to be rubbed out because they are not genuine expressions of a different professional ethos (as with your audit people compared with your field sales team). They can be simply remnants of a competing culture. Lord King had a problem in trying to reconcile the cultures of the two main entities that had come together to form British Airways – British European Airways (BEA) and the British Overseas Airways Corporation (BOAC). BEA operated a local taxi service to cities in Europe, as the BOAC people used to say, while BOAC flew flying boats on the old Empire routes to the colonies, as the BEA people used to say. Lord King was (still is) pretty charismatic himself and made short work of the differences, but this type of problem can be a killer. And the fact is that even the comparatively legitimate subcultures of, say, professional people operating in enclaves within a company can only be acceptable if they really do reflect aspects of the overall corporate culture. After all, although the field sales team are far more likely to deal with consumers on a daily basis, it is not unheard of for a consumer, or a journalist, to have dealings with a member of the audit staff. Woe betide the company if the conversation does not project the culture with which the consumer or journalist is already familiar.

Nothing is more destructive to a company's reputation and its chances of continuing commercial success than if its culture is divided against itself! The media love to hear from members of staff who deride their company's culture and who give the facts that justify the derision. The press calls them 'whistle-blowers'. The most notorious example of whistle blowing in recent years must be the still current outcry by insiders (and outsiders too) against organic foods. The culture/image of organic foods has developed naturally, as you would expect. The word 'organic' is a good word. The absence of 'chemical' fertilisers and pesticides is 'obviously a good thing'. And naturally, you'd expect to pay a little more because these healthy foods are grown by sons and daughters of the soil, toiling on their own small-holdings, without the mass-market facilities and funding of the factory farmers. What an image! What a culture to believe in and most of the organic food producers really think they live that culture every day of their lives. But hang on a minute. Here's someone who knows the business from the inside telling us that we, the consumers, are being ripped off, that the farmers here or in foreign parts who grow the organics, while genuinely ignoring those 'awful chemical pesticides and fertilisers' are applying unspeakable other things to the fruit and veg, possibly causing unpleasant effects on the innards of those innocents who eat them. And the prices are needlessly high too (husband to wife who has just unloaded the shopping on the kitchen table to reveal all her politically correct purchases: 'Organic, free-range, non-GM – d'you think we're made of money?').

The organic food industry is in danger of self-pollution, perhaps even self-destruction, because it has allowed its 'culture' to develop beyond the truth. Cultures not built on truth will fall, either because someone inside or someone outside blows the whistle. The walls of Jericho come to mind – they fell because someone blew the whistle (or trumpets in their case). Yet they seemed so strong.

Yes, cultures are complex things. At any rate, understanding the detail of one's own company's culture can seem complex. However, we can break it down into smaller parts, three of them in fact.

1. *'The Heart'*. It stands for the core elements of your culture; those derived from values, which are defined as 'ideals that have meaning to the company and its members'. When the values are shared values, they produce organisational beliefs ('assumptions which we all hold to be true') and in turn, these produce attitude (tendency to respond in a certain way). From the sum of these are derived norms (expected modes of behaviour). As an organisation evolves, these norms will produce outcomes which will become a feedback loop influencing the values → beliefs → norms and so on.

   For a corporate culture to form, a fairly stable group of people needs to have shared some history which has produced a social learning process. This is heavily influenced by the founder or early leaders in creating the culture. (Example: any advertising agency with the name Saatchi in its title is going to enjoy a culture for ever dominated by the personalities of the brothers.) Subsequent managers act as the 'culture carriers' reinforcing and socialising new people into the culture.

2. *'The wrapping'* is required to communicate the core elements so that newcomers understand and replicate the culture. It mediates the 'heart' of the culture and wraps it around with things that represent it. Often, this is about finding simple ways to describe more complex values. These are often found in stories, heroes and symbols, which carry messages about the core elements. (Leo Burnett, the advertising agency founder, was a diabetic. Stricken

during office hours by an attack that called for something sweet to be eaten, he was offered a piece of chocolate by an aide. 'Is it Hershey?', gasped Leo. It was, he ate it and recovered. Hershey was a Burnett client. Stories like this did the agency culture – and its image with clients and prospects – a power of good.)

3. *Distributing the 'virus'* is the final step, either formally or informally, in the distribution of a culture. Here, the organisation is trying to 'infect' or pass on the culture to newcomers. Formal methods include rituals, induction, training courses and appraisal systems. Informal methods include artefacts such as corporate work wear, physical space and common language. 'Socialisation' occurs as the individual learns to adapt his or her own values, beliefs, attitudes and norms in order to 'fit' in. Or leaves! Selection often reinforces this process by trying to find those who already seem to 'fit'.

In developing your 'All-to-One' culture you need to have a strong heart, a focal point around which the principles and philosophies can evolve and emanate. A strong champion, a leadership group can achieve this – perhaps even the trumpet call of 'All-to-One'. It is then that the wrappings, the techniques you use to protect, preserve the core of the heart will build momentum and the 'All-to-One' force will build from there. And widespread viral promulgation through the enterprise can begin.

Cultural values even when held by all members of management and staff can impede performance as well as support it. The latest example is Marks & Spencer, once the UK's greatest department store chain, the place where Mrs Thatcher is alleged to have bought her underwear, and where in fact a large chunk of the middle classes bought not just their underwear but their socks too. Every other type of garment was available, all good quality and all of respectable styling. You could also buy food. But you couldn't buy anything with a credit card, except that of the store – that's how confident they were. And you couldn't buy anything that wasn't in one way or another a St Michael product (St Michael was the Marks

& Spencer brand name) – that's how absolutely confident they were. But now ...! The conservative design of the stores, inside and outside, once yet another mark of confidence, became a symbol of out of dateness. The good taste of the clothes began to look safe, then dowdy. The absence of famous non-St Michael names turned off the brand-conscious younger buyers. In short, the cultural values that had propelled Marks & Spencer to the commanding heights are now pulling them down. Anyone who has loved Marks & Spencer since they first bought a pair of pants there will be delighted that the group is being brought up to date and revitalised. Let's hope that the Marks & Spencer culture and the values it enshrines get the treatment.

The culture of any company has to do the impossible – stay the same yet change with the times. Actually, it's not impossible. People do it all the time. You are the same person that you were 10 years ago. But look at photographs of yourself 10 years ago and marvel. Even more revealing, watch and listen to a movie/talkie of yourself taken 10 years ago. Is that really you? Yes. But you're still the same person. That's the now-you-see-it-now-you-don't change that your company's culture has to make over the years – assuming, of course, that the basic culture is the one you really want.

If it isn't, you'll want to change it, but how? Still with us Marks & Spencer?

Theoretically, since a culture is transmitted, learned and becomes part of a continuing social feedback loop, it should be possible to intervene in the loop and change it. However, cultures are inherently self-reinforcing and stable, which makes them tough to change. There seem to be four main constraints, outlined below.

Structure and technological

Much of the culture is embedded in the company's procedures, physical elements and documentation. As a result, short to medium-term change is difficult if not impracticable, even impossible. So, if you want to change the culture, you'd better start on the paper work.

Top-down culture change led by managers

Change engineered in this way is often resisted by employees. After all, why should they change? They joined the company in the first place because they liked its culture (not necessarily using that word). People in general dislike things being different.

I'm sorry to go on about Shell again, but it does seem to contain in microcosm (and not very micro either) the risks and rewards inherent in a strong culture.

Here's the relevance: when Mark Moody-Stuart became the top gun in Shell, the Group seemed likely to go into loss for the first time in its 100-year history. Low oil prices plus some comparatively unsuccessful investments were the immediate causes. Moody-Stuart diagnosed another, more fundamental reason – the Shell culture had become frozen in a 1970s/1980s mindset which assumed that by definition whatever Shell did was right. After all, Shell had more than its fair share of extremely bright people. But the culture needed a kick.

The sharp end of the kick took the form of a meeting to senior managers, hundreds of them, at which associated gurus, witch-doctors, mob orators, comedians and entertainers acted out in a series of *tableaux vivants* how fossilised Shell had become and how it had to loosen up. Uproar, not among those who attended, but among the chaps and chappesses back at the sites, or at least among some of them.

What are they playing at? What is Shell coming to? You can't produce oil out of a clown's hat! That sort of thing. But the culture has changed. And fortunately (for Shell's balance sheet) the price of oil has gone up. But no one is denying that the new Shell owes its make-over to initiative from the top, unwelcome though it may have been to some staff members. And no one is denying that it is the new Shell that can take advantage of the good things now on offer for it.

The culture change at Shell was accompanied by major structural changes – among them the dismantling of operating companies such as Shell UK and a merging of talents across country boundaries. The culture change went hand in hand with that.

Managers as barriers

Managers, having reached the top of their slippery pole, sometimes see no reason why they should change the nature of the pole. Their power and position depend on the existing culture, and its associated social system. Why change? So the required culture change finds powerful enemies. Managers have to be persuaded of the need for change if they haven't already seen the need themselves.

What happens outside can count

The context in which the company operates can have an enormous effect on the company's culture and any attempt to change it. I've already mentioned both the environment and the problems of the Third World as potent conditioners of attitudes and therefore of culture. Other considerations include such hot potatoes as gender, race, excess profit, the price of raw materials, war, stock market crashes, sundry panics such as the Y2K thing which had people prophesying *Apocalypse Now*, or at least on 1 January 2000, plus the considerations that no one's thought of yet.

Outside events can have a beneficial effect on a company's culture. That book by Ralph Nader, *Unsafe at any Speed*, seen first of all as an attack on the motor industry, has proved a benefaction. Other factors have been at work – the total quality management boom of the 1980s and ever-accelerating manufacturing efficiency brought about by the on-going computer revolution – but Nader's book pushed safety right into the heart of every motor manufacturer's culture.

On a similar world-shattering scale was Rachel Carson's wonderful book *Silent Spring*. When it was published in 1963 it did enormous damage to the reputation of the pesticide manufacturers and killed off whole swathes of products (ever heard of Dieldrin?). But the book etched one word into the culture of every chemical company. That word was safety. Safety of product and in manufacture is now taken for granted as the prime responsibility of the manufacturer – or should be, which itself is a vast improvement on the 'disasters are bound to happen occasionally' attitudes of previous generations of manufacturers. Chemical plant safety is now overwhelmingly dominant in the chemical companies' culture and, what is equally important, in the culture of every member of the public – so far as the public ever thinks about chemical plant safety. But the public does think about it when there is a disaster at a plant – and simply cannot understand how it could happen. This means that a disaster like the Bhopal explosion at the Union Carbide pesticide factory with its horrifying loss of life came as a terrible shock. Disasters on a similar scale had happened before. There was one in the UK at the chemical plant at Flixborough in 1974 when 28 people were killed and 36 injured. And there were many more. But the Bhopal explosion, although possibly it was the work of a disgruntled employee, happened when the safety culture was thought to be in charge. The only benefit to emerge – and it is an important one – is that the safety culture in the chemical companies was clearly not fully in charge and that still more effort was needed.

These are all outside events, of the direst kind, creating some good by strengthening the resolve of the people who run the chemical companies to improve the safety culture still more.

Other influential outside events have been less traumatic, though in some cases more far-reaching in their effect. The total quality management boom of the 1980s was just such an event and spawned all today's quality-through-zero-defects programmes.

The basic point about outside events is that they are outside your power to control or even prepare for. That's another reason why a 'one-to-one' approach to creating a company culture is painfully inadequate. *Everything* has to be taken into your reckoning, including the certainty of some kind of outside influence and the possibility of some kind of disaster.

The comfort is that a culture based on the 'All-to-One' principles is extremely resilient and can cope far more competently with whatever is thrown at it.

I end with some good news. You don't have to think of changing your current culture. Merely think of creating new values to add to your existing culture. As with everything to do with 'All-to-One', the process is evolutionary.

The other bit of good news is that all the other things you do with RelModel, the development of the capabilities for your marketing communications, the development of leadership, the greater understanding of your consumers, the RelTechnics I detailed earlier, the Journey Map which can be seen at the back of the book, the enterprise architecture I describe in the next chapter – all these will help your people in the development of your 'All-to-One' culture.

Mini case study

Tennessee truckers as ambassadors

EVERITT EXPRESS IS a Tennessee-based trucking company. Nothing sensational about it except its trucks are magnificently maintained, its schedules are inviolate, its promises are kept and, oh yes, its drivers act as if they own the company. Trouble brewing? The nearest driver will shoot it. Extra initiative needed? The driver on hand will provide it. Everitt Express has achieved this happy state, happy for company, drivers and consumers, by empowering its staff to think of themselves as ambassadors for their company. It's 'All-to-One' in a comparatively straightforward business-to-business relationship. But in a tough, competitive and often lonely business, it gets things done.

The importance of professional accreditation

'ALL-TO-ONE' IS NOT an easy option. Its full profitable application relies on the flair, energy, experience and professional know-how of the marketers. The first two characteristics are God-given. The next you can only earn over time. But you can do something now about the fourth (you've probably already done it). Professional qualifications are essential components in the armoury of a successful marketer. They demonstrate that you have a sound grasp of marketing essentials – and they won't change.

These essentials need to be built into the sinews of the organisation. They give it strength and gravity (these guys are serious, they mean business). They also show clients and CEOs that marketing is not something you pick up as you go along. You have to work at it and an apprenticeship is worthwhile. Those new web-page creatives and net-savvy young executives are not going to be properly equipped for their ambitions without a firm foundation in the grammar of business and basic marketing techniques. I have been very lucky learning from so many dedicated business leaders, business practitioners, committed and passionate marketers.

Others in many organisations are not going to be so lucky. There needs to be a concerted effort in all organisations to provide this type of apprenticeship, to provide role models/mentors, to create a passion for learning about the profession/trade/business of marketing. It's worth creating this environment of continuous and formal learning, even if some of the people you've invested in go off after three years to support another company. We all have a duty to spread the knowledge and the expertise. No one gained in anything but the short term by keeping knowledge to themselves. Besides, that brilliant young marketer whose training cost you a fortune might be offering you a well-paid directorship in his company one day.

There are broadly four ways of acquiring professional qualifications:

❏ a full-time course lasting two or three years at a university, college or business school

❏ a part-time course at any of the above – which will mean taking time off from work at fairly regular intervals

❏ evening classes

❏ a correspondence course.

Details of all these options, all of them available locally, can be found on the Internet.

Professional marketing and training organisations are more than willing to immerse themselves with you in training challenges – so go to it, involve them. They have great resources, great philosophies just waiting to be utilised in the real world of marketing.

Create libraries in your organisation of all the best current books (I've listed some of them later in the book); send your people on all the conferences and encourage them to join the relevant professional organisations. Only then are you 'walking the talk' and only then are you being other-centred.

Professional accreditation is a sign that you are taking 'All-to-One' seriously, that you are going to call on all the tools that you need to create a new consumer-focused strategy.

Marketing is now an accepted discipline in practically every university and college, as it always has been, of course, in the business schools. In addition there are the specialist marketing institutes, nearly all of which offer training followed by qualifications. In the UK, for instance, there are the Institute of Direct Marketing and the Chartered Institute of Marketing (both of which I am a member). But the Internet will give you names and contact numbers.

'All-to-One' education in Asia and elsewhere

London Chamber of Commerce and Industry Examinations Board show the way

MILLIONS OF SUCCESSFUL business people in all parts of the world, but particularly in Europe and the Asia/Pacific rim, gained their qualifications from the London Chamber of Commerce and Industry's Examinations Board (LCCIEB). Under arrangements that have held for more than a century, students receive specialist training from 'Centres' which can be either independent educational establishments or the training departments of large organisations. Syllabuses are co-ordinated by the Centres and LCCIEB together, the students take LCCIEB examinations and, if they pass, receive LCCIEB qualifications. With the role of the Centres so pivotal, LCCIEB's marketing effort to date has been directed primarily at them.

Times are changing, and LCCIEB is as aware as anyone of the education potential of the Internet and the opportunities it offers for direct links with students – who will be able to register directly, receive instruction, guidance and encouragement, interact with their tutors, and finally receive their qualifications – all directly through the Net. It's a kind of 'All-to-One-All' in action, since now all the resources of LCCIEB can be directed at the individual student who can respond to the mentor or anyone else in LCCIEB.

That's the idea in outline. Liam Swords, LCCIEB Chief Executive, paints a larger picture. 'It's in everyone's interests that the Net's education potential should be used to the full. But it's going to augment, not supplant existing arrangements. For instance, the Centres will continue to prosper, but through the Internet we'll be able to interact with people who don't have easy access to a Centre – and we can do it very cost-effectively. We'll offer training as well, something we haven't done before, plus a personal on-screen mentor for each student. The Net will help in another way. For the first time, we can communicate directly and interactively with the tutors.'

But Liam adds a caution: 'I think that if we confined our appearance to the Internet, our reputation in the community as a whole and with the educational establishment would suffer. The LCCIEB brand is very strong. We shall continue to back it in all the media at our disposal.'

Ten

'All-to-One' enterprise architecture

T HERE ARE TWO on-going essentials for an 'All-to-One' enterprise. The first is to ensure that everyone in the enterprise has a consumer-facing attitude. In the preceding chapters we've discussed what has to be done to achieve such an attitude.

The second essential is to ensure that the structure of the enterprise enables everyone to maintain and implement that consumer-facing attitude. By structure, I mean the way the enterprise organises its systems and processes, the way its people work, the way they are recognised and rewarded, and the way the enterprise as a whole functions – in a phrase: the enterprise architecture.

This chapter shows how such an architecture can be developed in your enterprise.

A consumer-centric strategy – an 'All-to-One' strategy – requires a consumer-centric enterprise architecture. Everything in the enterprise has to be consumer-centric, your infrastructure and systems, your marketing operations, your service delivery, your chief executive, particularly your chief executive. Without this 'enterprise architecture', you will not get the right responses from your people, or the right focus for their work, you will not get the right consumer data, the right information at the right time to service a consumer properly, you will not be able to turn your company into a learning organisation. In fact there's no end of things you won't be able to do, because it is your enterprise architecture that keeps your organisation facing towards the consumer, and it is the consumer that will make your organisation a success.

Let me issue a polite warning to all CEOs out there: you'll cripple your own best efforts to create an 'All-to-One' enterprise architecture in your organisation if you allow the ROI and cost-reduction mindset to win the day. That mindset, obsessed with short-term return, has led too many good companies in the wrong direction. You have to act for the longer term. An enterprise architecture supporting a consumer-facing 'All-to-One' strategy will be paying back for tens of decades to come and will secure your company's future, your own future and the future of those who come after you (towards the middle of the century, I mean).

None of this can be evaluated in terms of two-and-a-half year cost-reduction payback cycles and the like. Take a look at the financial markets' payback cycles for the dotcoms for a guide. An 'All-to-One' enterprise architecture needs investment. Do not even flirt with a consumer-centric strategy unless you are prepared to invest. All you will do is take focus off any alternative strategy you may have in mind for your organisation. Half-hearted attempts are a waste of money, time and effort. Take a hard look at what you want and treat your enterprise like those dotcom start-ups: give it the investment it needs, not the investment you would like – and certainly not the investment determined by other issues like this year's IT budget. And remember we're talking about a comprehensive investment, not just money but your time, your emotions, your energy – your job.

So what is involved when you set about creating an 'All-to-One' enterprise architecture in your organisation? I have the following key elements on my checklist:

1. Consumer-centric organisation

2. Enterprise consumer processes

3. Integrated marketing operations

4. Enterprise data architecture

5. The learning organisation

1. Consumer-centric organisation

Your organisation should exist to champion the consumer not to provide a framework for corporate politics. If the most powerful people in the company are financial specialists, or engineers, or research scientists, or, please not, the 'politicians', none of them with a heritage of consumer service or an interest in it, then, to state the obvious, your organisation is not consumer-centric, because when push comes to shove, the people with the biggest shove have a mindset that does not put consumers first.

Being consumer-centric for many will mean re-engineering the whole organisation around the consumer. This new orientation cannot just be about improving discrete parts of the organisation to serve consumers better but re-engineering the whole to provide an integrated consumer-centric enterprise where processes flow seamlessly to the consumer's benefit across what used to be traditional unconnected silos.

One way to help your company look outwards rather than at its own navel is to segment your consumers into groups and appoint 'champions' in the company who are empowered to re-engineer key processes within their divisions to support better a particular consumer group. Example: if you can identify the over 50s as an important consumer group, give the internal champion authority to influence all processes and interactions with that group, including the product, packaging and price, in the interests of that group. You might end up with a new range of revenue generators!

Other teams in the company, without specific consumer groups to champion, should be defined as support teams – they support those groups who *do* have consumers to champion. You could go further, and attach all staff without a consumer responsibility to those groups who do have one.

You can strengthen this whole consumer-facing re-engineering movement by getting the consumer-group champions to report regularly to senior management and staff. How is the company managing its consumers? Are the service levels being achieved or upgraded? What are the problems that consumers are facing? What have been our solutions? Reporting on new learning opportunities and new consumer initiatives should be part of the whole exercise. This should not be propaganda. The positives as well as the negatives should be openly and honestly shared with the rest of the organisation.

Different kinds of organisational concepts and methodologies abound but I particularly like the concept of the inverted pyramid (which I have mentioned before) with the consumer service teams at the top and the CEO at the bottom, holding the company on his or her shoulders. The pyramid concept is a useful way of getting rid of the normal hierarchies that people build into organisational structures (your boss is above you, your boss's boss is above your boss and so on upwards and downwards). The inverted pyramid structure has the consumer basking at the top, with the consumer-service teams in attendance. Beneath them are the support groups, and beneath them the groups supporting the support groups and eventually, finally the CEO. So everybody in the organisation is supporting the consumer-service people. Anyone who is not is redundant.

Redundant? Tough?

Another way of looking at this redundancy point is to say that if you cannot define your role in respect of a consumer then it is your role that is redundant. Tough? Not really. Business is crying out for people with the insight and honesty to admit that their role has no consumer relevance. You'll soon find one that has, because the overall answer is to redefine all job roles in terms of the consumer, even though the job may only have a support or back office role.

Another suggestion, symbolic maybe, but I know it works, is to change all job titles to include the word 'consumer'. You could re-name the research department the Consumer Learning Support Team and define its role as not only to carry out research but also to be responsible for communicating its research findings to everyone in the organisation and particularly the consumer contact staff. The research people in fact become the champions of organisational understanding and of getting closer to the company's consumers. Accounts Receivable could be re-named the Consumer Transaction Support Team – its goal would be to see consumer transactions from the point of view of the consumer.

Keep on asking yourself: Why are we organised like this? How relevant is the way that we're organised to the way we would like to do business? What really are our goals? How does our market strategy strengthen our consumer 'touch points'? What signals are we giving to our staff on value priorities? Are you a boss or a manager? Are you a boss or a leader? Are you a boss or a liberator of your consumer-facing teams?

Never underestimate the influence of your organisational architecture on your people's attitude to the company and the consumers. How many bosses have you worked for who have prioritised managing inwards (to service their bosses) rather than focusing outwards (to service their consumers) and so encouraging staff to do the same. We all recognise bosses who have made such a fetish of monthly sales figures to the extent of massaging them (tut, tut), before disappearing upstairs for the management drinks party. Does politics get you promoted in your organisation – or championing the consumer? The correct answers are obvious – correct that is from the point of view of the consumer-led and success-seeking organisation. But are they the answers you are getting in your company today?

2. Enterprise consumer processes

This is all about having all of your consumer 'touch points' known and understood by each type of consumer. Once you understand consumer buying behaviour and offered the consumer a range of different ways of interacting with you (Internet, telephone, face to face, direct mail, whatever), you can design the processes around those different ways to deliver a satisfying and profitable relationship. You can then present one and the same face to consumers whichever of the touch points they prefer to use.

Achieving an organisation that is oriented around the profitable interaction with consumers through multiple channels, all of them consumer-centric, is no easy task. Getting there cannot be a half-hearted effort. It will require leadership from the very top of the organisation (or the bottom if you've achieved the inverted pyramid!).

The first phase in developing a consumer-centric organisation is major re-engineering. Usually this is a radical redesign of the existing organisational processes – driven by the need to serve and satisfy consumers more effectively. The key drivers for re-engineering will be dramatic improvements in quality of service, in speed of service, and in cost of service. Re-engineering in this instance is not about incremental changes or improvements that enable consumer focus, but about starting from scratch, designing whole new integrated processes that will manage the consumer relationship more effectively and more profitably. If radical action is needed, then be bold and take it – before your competitors do.

Re-engineering starts and finishes with the consumer – supporting the consumer, creating the most effective ways of serving the consumer. As my wife (Sue Luengo-Jones I should say) always says with her sales hat on, 'put yourself in the buyers' shoes, imagine what turns them on, see the world from their perspective, imagine what works for them – and then give it to them' (quite simple really). The processes should then be designed around this view of the world – ignoring all the old platitudes and inertia. Basically you should start again, forget the past and the politics of the past, ignore the old certainties, start again with the consumer.

In short, don't re-engineer an old process. Examine what the consumer needs and how best to satisfy those needs. And go for major improvements not just incremental change.

One great side benefit here is that when redefining your processes you can use all the latest technologies to become more efficient. You must ensure improvements in quality, service and speed of delivery as well as cut costs.

As we discussed in the previous chapter, take on board a number of change-agent behaviours and integrate them into your new enterprise consumer processes. Look at elements such as your task-based, process-based activities; ask yourself: 'What can I outsource?', 'How can the processes reshape the organisation?', 'Do the new processes replace specialists with generalists? Break all the rules. Use IT, then some more. Think total quality management.

Here are some other throwaway items to get your mind in the right groove:

❑ Combine several jobs into one.

❑ Let the workers make decisions.

❑ Make sure work is carried out where it makes most sense (for example, if you're a haulage company, get the trucks serviced where they happen to be – don't insist they come back to base).

❑ Empower your consumer service representatives.

❑ Promote on the basis of performance and ability.

❑ Project your values and beliefs throughout the enterprise.

❑ Transform managers from supervisors to coaches ...

❑ ... and executives from scorekeepers into leaders.

❑ Integrate processes to create multidimensional jobs and organise them into process teams.

Be on your guard: when a company re-engineers, jobs will change, relationships between workers and managers will change, so will career paths, so will what goes on in people's heads.

A recent survey in North America showed that 77 per cent of service industry companies had consumer care programmes but less than 20 per cent actually believed that they had any impact on performance or shareholder value. The key is that many of them actually only measured internal metrics rather than connecting to the perception of quality of service with the consumers. Many companies have adopted quality programmes that have not taken in all parts of the organisation and not embraced total enterprise quality and an 'All-to-One' responsibility. The key weaknesses have been the lack of motivational effort and other organisational issues.

One of the most important elements within a re-engineering exercise is the change in value systems of your people. Everything that is done must be related back to the profitable satisfaction of consumers – other values held that get in the way of this will be diluted or eradicated over time. You should set up new reward systems and well-directed incentive schemes. All these will help focus people's minds and aspirations on the values desired by the organisation – the performance metrics that relate to consumers and consumers' satisfaction. People will be empowered to make the right decision on behalf of the consumer. These decisions will be driven by new attitudes to the consumer, installed through a new corporate culture.

Appoint 'All-to-One' champions

Achieving the level of change required in the first phase of re-engineering will require the support of the most senior management within the organisation. In addition, a key individual must be found to play the role of the 'All-to-One' champion. The 'All-to-One' champion must be senior enough to make change happen, must be able to break down the old barriers, change the structures and the old reward systems. He/she must be a visionary, ambitious and a motivator with authority over how things happen in the organisation. The champion will be a passionate advocate of the 'All-to-One' concept – otherwise it will be a re-engineering programme for the sake of it. The single objective must be about better satisfying consumers through an 'All-to-One' culture, organisation and continuous learning initiative. The 'All-to-One' champion will use the RelModel to assess where the organisation currently is in terms of consumer relationship maturity and define the high-level goals for adopting the next stages on the RelModel. The 'All-to-One' champion will be responsible for a comprehensive audit to identify organisational readiness and to identify the actions that lie ahead which will form the planned journey up the RelModel.

Supporting the 'All-to-One' champion will be a number of process owners. The 'All-to-One' champion will appoint the process owners. These process owners will have enough seniority to effect change within their division. They will need the authority to discard the old task-oriented roles and re-assign people to new roles within new integrated processes. The process owners will set the objectives for developing an 'All-to-One' environment and ensure that the objectives are met through the constant evaluation and monitoring of the programme.

In turn re-engineering teams will support the process owners. These teams will be made up of ambitious members from a number of disciplines within the organisation. These teams will map out how the new processes will support the integrated marketing concepts within the RelModel.

Together the 'All-to-One' champion, the process owners and the re-engineering teams will reshape and refocus the organisation to adopt the RelModel concept. This will ensure that the organisation moves along the maturity model faster than its competitors and as a result creates more powerful consumer relationships and improved competitive positioning.

3. Integrated marketing operations

The achievement of an 'All-to-One' organisation will be helped immeasurably by ensuring that marketing processes are integrated. This integration is essential in moving on from Level 1 of the RelModel. Many opportunities to re-engineer the marketing processes may be found within the integrated marketing model (IMM). The IMM represents a series of processes to ensure that the organisation moves to a consumer-centric focus and can constantly improve its consumer understanding, consumer relationships, consumer satisfaction and the ability to surprise and delight.

The IMM has five distinct and easy-to-understand processes, which act as guides to focusing your marketing operations on the cycles required for improving your consumer-focus capability:

Five-stage integrated marketing model

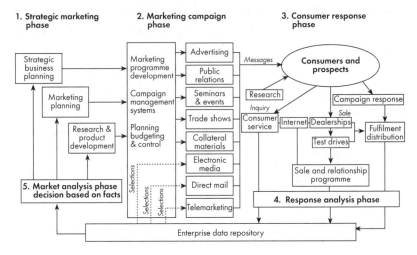

❑ the strategic planning phase

❑ the campaign execution phase

❑ the consumer response phase

❑ the campaign measurement phase

❑ the market analysis phase

The IMM is for the whole organisation but most crucially for the marketing practitioners, the marketing operations team who have to make things happen in this space. The diagram above illustrates five key processes of the virtuous learning cycle of the IMM. It uses an integrated approach from initial strategy through to execution, where the flows of activity and information have clear dependency on each other. It also shows how, through continuous measurement, feedback and modification, your marketing operations can keep you ahead of the competition.

Strategic planning phase

On the left of the model is the strategic planning process, which is where amongst other things you would create the 'All-to-One'

Journey Map (covered in the pull-out section on the inside back cover) and is where tools such as RelTechnics, the consumer and market research methodology described in Chapter 5, would be used.

If you are a consumer-facing company, how do you connect with what is in the minds of your consumers, with their emotions towards your product or service? And how do you connect this to your communications and your operations? In this process, you answer these questions. You may well end up with a comprehensive journey map – such as the 'All-to-One' Journey Map prepared by John Caswell at the back of this book. This is very much the 'What are you going to do' phase.

At this phase, you would:

❑ Determine your strategic direction, basing it on the requirements of corporate planning.

❑ Evaluate the marketplace – your consumers.

❑ Segment the market.

❑ Determine the expectations of the consumers you intend to lock into.

In short, you work to gain the enlightened edge over your competition in the marketplace.

This is very much the thinking and defining direction part of the IMM. Your decisions, I hope, will be based on fact, but we will come to that point on our way around the virtuous IMM cycle.

Campaign execution phase

This phase covers both campaign planning and campaign execution. Here you need to set and document the campaign goals and to associate detailed metrics against which the campaign can be measured in a later phase of the integrated cycle. If the campaign is not properly set up in either the planning or execution stage, then you will not be able to maximise your learning from your campaigns.

In this phase, you set up any control groups needed to evaluate the different impacts to the different groups of your campaigns. You also decide with your fulfilment teams what processes are needed to capture response, or with the research teams what research needs to be done, how it is going to be done and what consumer perception change criteria need to be used.

Whereas the strategic planning phase was dominated by analysis, here planning, processes and creative execution dominate the thinking and decision making. You would be identifying the right media to match your consumers' behaviour, moods, modes and decision-making processes identified when you implemented the 'Getting closer to your consumer through the RelTechnics' in the strategic planning process. You would also taking into account the 'transformation' techniques described in the special section entitled 'A vision of what might be'.

Once you have selected your media and developed your campaigns, you can start to execute them (easier said, I appreciate, than done).

Consumer response phase

In this phase, you send messages out to your consumers and expect a response of some kind. If you are looking for a change in perception, you should research your campaign to determine its impact. If there is a response mechanism in the campaign, you will need to monitor the take-up through your fulfilment channels. Other reactions will come through existing channels – your sales force, the distribution or retail departments, the consumer-enquiry people, or indeed any part of the company or extended organisation with consumer-facing responsibilities.

It is crucial that the metrics that you set up in the campaign planning phase are now in place and all response is captured and measured. A great deal of care should be taken to collate every response. For example, with a mailing, you must evaluate the reasons why people didn't respond, as well as the number of people who did. Test segments and other control groups set up to provide proper evaluation data need to be tracked along with ensuring that data collection processes are implemented and maintained at every consumer touch point.

Response analysis phase

Provided you have prepared the ground in the set up of your campaigns and in the collection of all the data in the consumer response process, the response analysis phase can provide you with the reasons for your success (or failure) and indicate the lessons to be learned from this cycle of your marketing operations. The response analysis phase helps you achieve better targeting, improved media selection and improved consumer communications in the future. This is the key source from which the consumer understanding, the campaign expertise and experience are gained. It will help you to move from Level 1 in the RelModel (inhabited by the 'spray and pray' brigade) to Level 2 and at Level 2 acquire the capabilities that will take you to Level 3 and so forth.

Market analysis phase

The lessons learned from these campaigns and the extra data now feeding into the enterprise database enable you to make more enlightened market analysis than was possible before the end of the first cycle – just as the various learning stages of the RelModel can bring you to a greater understanding of your consumer and provide you with the ability to move up to Levels 3 and 4. There may be several campaign and data-gathering cycles to move you up to the next level of the RelModel. This would be the same with the 'All-to-One' Journey Map at the back of this book. You may have to do more than one or two versions of the 'All-to-One' Journey Map before you are able to move up to a new level of consumer relationship maturity. The analysis at this phase is deeper than the analysis of campaign activity. Your analysis is now based on direct experience with your marketplace, your consumers. Provided the right questions were designed into the campaigns and the right metrics in place, all the consumer interactions with the company during the campaign can be linked to the enterprise data architecture. They will then provide the basis for future decisions both in the strategic planning process and the campaign creation processes to be based on fact.

4. Enterprise data architecture

One of the most effective enablers available to the 'All-to-One' consumer-focused enterprise is the effective application of new technologies. This application is used in the search for fast, flexible and cost-effective distribution and interaction channels with consumers as well as to support the analysis and management of markets, consumers and individual consumer relationships.

Information technology can be a real asset but has become a major roadblock for many organisations, with IT and business functions feuding over the management and application of IT services. In this section I would like to explain how different types of technologies can be employed to support the integrated marketing model. These technologies should form part of the new re-engineered 'All-to-One' organisational model. The concepts below should help in the creation of re-engineered processes to support dramatically improved consumer relationships and organisational effectiveness.

As the diagram on page 241 indicates, these various components must come together to form the enterprise consumer management architecture.

Enterprise consumer data model

The data model needs to be flexible. It should contain the data you need not the data you happen to have. Which data is needed will depend on your strategic plan and the key levers that drive that strategic plan. The data for those key levers to drive the plan and drive the organisation to achieve the plan must be contained in the data model.

You need to create an environment with a culture of collaboration, where 'consumer interactions', whatever their source, are

Enterprise consumer management architecture

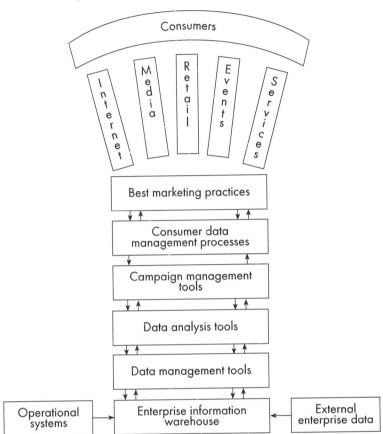

monitored, assessed for quality and where appropriate, stored. Quality assessment is vital, and the criteria for consumer assessment should be rigorous (I list them below). Numerous household-name companies (names on request) collect mountains of information and wonder what to do with it. They should scrap them and start again.

The enterprise data model should contain the information to answer at a minimum the following questions:

Criteria for consumer assessment

❑ Who are they?

❑ What have they bought?

❑ What problems have they had (and, importantly, what did we do about them, and when)?

❑ What might they want to buy?

❑ How important are they to my company?

❑ How vulnerable are they to my competition?

The fundamental principles are that you must have an enterprise-wide view of the type of information you collect about your consumers and that all operational and transactional data must be consolidated into one central database − the only place where all enterprise data ends up.

Don't allow departments to have their own independent silos with their own consumer and marketing communications databases. Such silos are guaranteed to deliver poor consumer service. How could they not? Good consumer service requires the consumer to be recognised and treated in the same way by every part of the enterprise. After all, the consumer who receives a mail shot, or logs on to your website, or rings to get special information remains the same person. The company should remain the same company. A multiplicity of information sources lead to unacceptable variations in the messages and impressions received by the consumer. It also leads to consumers − and opportunities − being overlooked. What a waste of your marketing communications budget! Without an enterprise-wide view and an enterprise-wide use of all your data, you have no chance of moving up through the RelModel levels.

Consumer management, of course, must extend throughout the entire consumer/company relationship, from the first casual enquiry through to lifelong membership/partnership. Every casual enquiry must be followed up, for the good reason that it could be the beginning of a lifelong relationship, which could maximise value for both sides. Once someone − consumer or non-consumer − has contacted you, he or she becomes a prospective consumer whom you can reach out to. A prospective consumer is far more worthwhile than a consumer using another brand, or not using any brands in the category, or a consumer with no intention of contacting you.

Without a consolidated source of relevant and detailed consumer information, answers to such questions are difficult to assemble on demand and may be difficult to act upon. It is not possible for your people to give consistent service or provide one face to the consumer without a robust enterprise data architecture.

One information source, many marketing uses

Consolidated consumer information may be used for many purposes. It can help profile existing consumers, identify high-value prospects, compare the effectiveness of different campaigns, direct the shape of advertising campaigns, facilitate everyday communication with consumers through letters, e-mails and telephone calls.

The bedrock reason for maintaining a one-only consolidated information source in your company is that everyone in your company works with and from the same consumer information.

Consumer data warehouses and data marts

Consumer data warehouses are comprehensive reservoirs of information, planned around the questions that the company needs to ask of consumer data. Consumer data marts allow you to ask questions that relate to your strategic intentions and your tactical execution, your segmentation strategy, your distribution strategy, your campaign programmes and so forth.

Consumer data marts are fed from the data warehouse with the subset of information required to answer the specific question. Information within a data mart may therefore be summarised, or aggregated from the information held within the underlying data warehouse. For example, a data mart might exist to identify an organisation's most profitable consumers, or to identify the demographic profile of the consumers of an organisation's most profitable product, or its most effective media for advertisement response. Data marts represent your different treatment of a segment and as you move up the levels of RelModel you will need subsets of information that enable more sophisticated handling of particular consumer groups.

The approach to consumer decision support systems is to develop data marts as they are actually to be used with particular consumer groups, for particular strategic initiatives to support your consumer-facing framework. They should be populated from the main consumer data warehouse, and not directly from operational systems. The individual data marts should be married against your organisational structure and as such should be married against the consumer-centric strategy and as such against consumer groups, supported by consumer champions.

Experience has shown that population from a central database, and not from operational systems directly, is the most efficient way to build these solutions in the longer term:

The best kind of data architecture...

❏ is planned and repeatable and follows industry-best practice

❏ uses iterative, disciplined processes, gradually adding layers of detail but delivering initial benefits fast

❏ is business focused, existing solely to improve the business

❏ involves and empowers the whole enterprise in its projects, not only IT projects using the latest technology, but also projects that involve business sponsors from the outset so as to ensure a 'by-the-business-for-the-business' focus

❏ applies the technology realistically, that is the scope is kept realistic, focused on business benefits.

Operational data

Systems in the operational environment create and maintain the data required in the running of the business. The data collected probably has wide applicability to the enterprise as a whole. However, it is likely to be collected and held in a form that is optimised for the needs of the specific application. Data at this level can be considered as current, transactional information required to run the business – whom to invoice, who has paid, what are the current stock levels, etc.

Operational data is typically:

❏ business process oriented

❏ oriented to a single business function

❏ current, with high volatility (they are highly likely to change)

❏ mostly at a transaction level

❏ often available in real time

❏ with limited historical content.

Watch out for independent and silo consumer operational databases; they are a sure sign of fragmentation of the company in the eyes of the consumer, a sure sign of problems lying in wait for your consumers. Application databases provide the mechanism for the creation and retention of data, and its use in applications that support business processes. They typically fulfil specific business needs, and hence often require 'application-specific' data that has limited scope across the enterprise. Often the data model is designed with a narrow scope in mind. Typically the business department responsible for a function has collected 'operational data', and therefore a departmental view and a sense of ownership has developed. This in turn has meant that the true value of that information is not shared across the enterprise.

Enterprise databases

Enterprise databases provide an integrated, common 'reference database' for critical data objects. These enterprise databases act as the source for information that is commonly shared across the extended organisation. Your data is precious and when organised for the consumer is the information you need to run the business.

Data warehouses are the consolidation and storage of atomic level data with a fine level of granularity. Data warehouses hold a nonvolatile view of data in the enterprise. Data is maintained at a low level of detail; data retention and history are deep.

The data stores represent the database designs, models, and physical data elements that provide the means to deliver complete, timely, accurate, and understandable business information to individuals for effective decision making. Providing information to drive strategic decision making is the key element behind the design of these data stores.

With data marts the information is organised around a subject area, the data is optimised around a specific set of business questions, that is, it is optimised around usage. The design of these stores is driven by specific functional business requirements, data access and performance. There is less data and faster access for specific tasks designed around operational needs. The scope of the data maintained in the data marts is a subset of the data contained in the data warehouse. When business pressure mandates a data mart to be built first, it should form the foundation stone of a warehousing strategy.

Additionally, the cost of interfaces is much greater with a data mart-only strategy: with 5 source systems feeding 5 data marts there needs to be 25 interfaces, 25 cleansing routines and so on. When the first direct data mart in a direct marketing strategy is created there seems to be no problem. A direct data mart-only strategy is industry worse practice, and costs more in the long run.

With a warehousing strategy feeding 5 data marts from 5 source systems requires 10 interfaces; furthermore the data is available within a warehouse to be re-used.

This is all nitty gritty stuff, but it's vitally important!

Data cleansing and transformation

Information within an organisation often grows on a department-by-department basis, and commercial pressures have often meant that little consideration has been given to the wider requirements of the enterprise. In turn this gives rise to inconsistency of quality, standards and formatting.

Even if standards were once defined, they have likely changed with time, without retrofitting the older applications to match the new standards. In the case of applications purchased from outside, there is often no externally defined standard to which they comply and hence no consistency between them, and seldom even within them.

This lack of standards for the data in existing applications means that there is little value in providing direct access to the data.

A common attitude is that 'Our data is already good quality' – while the truth is that data is nearly always inconsistent, particularly when multiple information silos are involved.

If you take it seriously, then you need to put the right team on it and the representatives from all aspects of consumer-facing enterprise data architecture and back operations need to be included.

The enterprise data architecture exists to solve real issues and to improve the business; and active early participation from the business ensures that it is not driven by IT.

When business pressure mandates a data mart to be built first, it should form the foundation stone of a data warehousing strategy. Quite often politics, empire building or sheer inertia in an enterprise mean that departments are forced to go it alone – resulting in the proliferation of data and a fragmented data architecture and an enterprise not focused or co-ordinated around the consumer.

Quick wins on the road to the big picture are fine and encouraged. Smaller projects such as departmental data marts can fit within the 'All-to-One' enterprise architecture as long as you adopt a data warehouse strategy so that smaller projects can fit in today and be started tomorrow – do not wait as there are always the smaller non-strategic projects all over every organisation.

The architecture provides the foundation for consistent terminology and architecture across all data management and warehousing efforts. It also focuses project teams to agree scope and functionality based on a common understanding, and to leverage experiences of components (e.g. processes, designs, tools and functions) and data (e.g. designs, models and data). In order to support this re-use, the database contains details of reusable components, experiences and recommendations.

The 'All-to-One' enterprise data architecture comprises five elements:

❏ operational data

❏ data staging areas

❏ data warehouses

❏ data marts

❏ decision support.

A key fundamental principle of 'All-to-One' enterprise architecture is to grow a centralised enterprise database or warehouse with each successive project, so that we start with the end in mind. This approach means that the warehouse is only as large as it needs to be to support the first data mart.

The analysis on how to populate the data mart needs to be performed for any data mart; but rather than lose that in the intricacies of an interface, our approach builds this into a reusable, scalable warehouse. A central warehouse has the benefit of making data within it a shared resource, as well as sharing data transformation and cleansing routines. The results of this strategy are that over time, the overall cost is less.

In the worst-case scenario a data mart-only policy is pursued without first defining the long-term strategy. Typically, depending on the systems used, different answers may be received from different systems to the same questions. In this scenario companies find themselves backtracking and putting in place a central data warehouse.

Here is an example of how this could happen:

The typical organisation is organised around vertical departmental functional areas. Typically these departments each have their own IT systems, in which departmental needs drive system developments. Because of commercial pressures, these developments were made at the expense of the wider needs of the organisation.

The result is that consumer information may well be scattered throughout the organisation's databases, making it difficult to access, and often impossible to summarise and aggregate.

Each part of the organisation could have its own identifier for the same consumer, and sense needs to be made of disparate sources of consumer information. Does this sound familiar? So how can sense be made of a consumer data landscape such as this?

Three steps towards an 'All-to-One' enterprise data architecture

The newly organised consumer-centric company needs to take a number of steps to migrate towards consumer-centric solutions:

1. *Step 1* – Assign a consumer data owner, empowered to decide what consumer data should be held. As previously mentioned the organisation decides what information is important to its consumer-centric strategy.

2. *Step 2* – Apply the newly defined consumer data standards to a database built to hold the consumer interactions. Decide how and what consumer data should be held. All new requirements for consumer data should be sourced using this database, while existing systems retain their consumer information for the time being. This approach allows good quality data to facilitate a decision support capability as soon as possible.

3. *Step 3* – Remove consumer data from existing disparate sources, eventually leaving only one source of consumer data. All consumer data requirements are now sourced from this new database.

This three-step process may take some time but do not be blown off course. If your consumer information is important to you then spend the money – get serious, invest or be resigned to uncontrolled consumer data, uncontrolled consumer relationships.

5. The learning organisation

A theme throughout this chapter is the concept of the 'virtuous learning cycle'. The cycle is virtuous because the more you learn, the more you find that there is to learn. As a result, the competence (and confidence) of your enterprise is on a continuous upward curve. The problem with many companies (and people too) is not what they don't know, but that they don't know what they don't know – which is why ignorance may be bliss in some walks of life, but certainly not in business.

A virtuous learning cycle ensures that continuous improvement is taken as normal and the standards of operational excellence are continually nudged upwards. Perpetual-learning organisations will keep moving up the RelModel levels and maintain their position at the level required. They will take on board the lessons learned at each level and put those lessons into effect at the next level. They will make sure that everyone in the enterprise is aware of the lessons – and of the mistakes, omissions and shortcomings that triggered them.

An effective learning organisation is one which has the confidence to make mistakes as it moves up through the five RelModel levels and not to blame those who make them (that's where the CEO comes in). It is one which values the 'understanding, feedback, learning, accountability' cycle. It is one that builds a service ethic into its culture and into the culture of all its agents and suppliers (the extended enterprise), and uses the ethic to incentivise consumers into becoming consumers and consumers into becoming lifelong 'partners'.

The learning organisation is then able to drive up quality standards continually to develop a sense of operational excellence, consistent service delivery with quality assurance and consumer feedback tied in.

The 'All-to-One' way of thinking encompasses both quality and consumer service, and shows how these can be managed and how any perception gap between what consumers expect and what they actually receive can be closed. The relationships with your consumers depend on the relationships within an organisation. The re-engineered enterprise consumer processes are the lynch pin to integrating those relationships to the good of the consumers. The shared internal values effectively become part of the products and services you provide.

At Johnson Matthey they learned the hard way that you have to get management's involvement not just their backing. Involved leadership is essential. Johnson Matthey did all the usual things. They set their quality programme up with high profile consultants, head office groups, regional committees and so forth. Head office led the way and each business unit was made accountable for the quality improvement process. Staff began to feel that all that senior management were doing was communicating the importance of the process without getting involved, not 'dirtying their hands' as my father used to say. Things began to fall into disrepute, especially when the stream of 'good news stories' through the official internal channels was not being reflected in local reality. Scepticism ensued. Following a review the company changed tack and the quality improvement process was put firmly into the hands of senior line management. Their involvement placed the quality improvement process firmly into their normal strategy planning process where quality planning, quality execution and quality control were now mandatory. There was no longer a need for the separate head office quality teams – the process was now fully integrated into the fabric of the organisation, into the normal processes for running the business. So, instead of it being a top-down head office idea, it was everyone's idea. The changes in behaviour were the result of changes in organisation.

Consider now an example where the idea of quality based on a learning process has pervaded the whole of the organisation, everyone in it. Historically the rise of Rank Xerox has been on the back of quality initiatives. Rank Xerox had a quality programme called 'Leadership through Quality'. It established a quality policy, strategic objectives with supporting standards, comprehensive guidelines and all the associated processes. The global plan was communicated as clear strategy and the quality policy stated:

'Xerox is a quality company. Quality is the basic business principle for Xerox. Quality means providing our external and internal consumers with innovative products and services that fully satisfy their requirements. Quality improvement is the job of every Xerox employee.'

At Rank Xerox the emphasis was on finding out who your consumer was (internal or external) and finding out what they expected from you. There was direct research down to individual consumer level – so employees could see that the answers and the requirements came direct from consumers and were not the daydreams of Xerox management. And because the answers were communicated to every employee, they became every employee's responsibility. Employees realised that they needed to change their attitudes and routines, even though at the time they thought they were answering consumer expectations. They realised that consumer expectations were always changing, always expecting better, and that competitors' own efforts were continually improving. The learning cycle became fully virtuous because everyone in the company could learn directly from the consumers and from consumers' experience of competitors. Everyone at Rank Xerox was involved in facing the consumer in learning about the consumer – or should I say All at Rank Xerox.

Companies that get organised and do all this by design will be the winners!

'All-to-One' with Toyota, El Monte, California

REG PENSKE RUNS the world's largest single Toyota dealer … the name, Longo … the place El Monte, California. Longo sells more than 25,000 cars each year. That's an enviable start to any case study. It gets better. Seventy per cent of those sales are repeat purchases from existing consumers. One reason why is the after care. Longo mechanics have his or her name on their 'office' – otherwise known as 'car repair stall'. Consumers know personally the mechanic who looks after their vehicle, and through the mechanic they have contact with the whole enterprise, and vice versa. Everyone at Longo has a focus on each consumer. It's not hype. It's just the way it is. It works.

The 'All-to-One' future

'ALL-TO-ONE' HAS BEEN with us since people first bought and sold things successfully. It will stay with us for as long as people *continue* to buy and sell things *successfully*. Which means there's a lot of 'All-to-One' future to come. So we'd better be modest and calibrate the crystal ball only as far forward as 2010. Most of us will still be around then, so we'll be able to have a good laugh of what I'm about to write – although at the time of writing I believe my forecasts to be reasonably well informed and reasonably likely to come about.

Here goes:

I forecast first, as a general and over-riding principle, that consumer focus will characterise every successful company – as, of course, it does now, except in 2010 there will be far more successful companies around and the focus will be far sharper. It will reveal more about the consumer to the company, it will enable the company to *mean* more to the consumer. It will track the dynamics of consumer preferences, as they change and develop. And it will be able to do that partly because of technological development – which, I also predict, will continue to amaze us – and partly because the people who run the company will realise much more than they do now that the consumer *is* their future. The culture change we discussed in Chapter 9 (Creating an 'All-to-One' culture in your company) will be the norm in every successful company and the urgent aim of every other (or should be).

As a result of this sharply increased consumer focus, there will be a distinct increase in consumer democracy. The 'All' in 'All-to-One' will be even more dedicated to the interests of the 'One', the whole system even more at the service of the consumer. What the consumer, the 'One', says, thinks, feels, complains about, is happy about, is apathetic about, all of that will become significant inputs to every successful company's decision-making process.

This will be democracy in action in a fully literal sense – consumers will dictate company policy and decisions by their actions, more particularly by their buying and usage behaviour, all of which will be meticulously, sensitively tracked by the new technologies. There will be no 'Big Brother is watching you' fears. The new technologies will only be used with permission – I agree thoroughly with Seth Godwin on the increasing importance of 'permission' in marketing. And they will be non-intrusive, for instance, computational technology embedded in domestic appliances will enable accurate measurement of consumer purchasing and consumption patterns without annoyance to anyone.

So, not only will products and services be more closely aligned to consumer needs and preferences, but also the consumers themselves will have a much greater and more direct influence on the way the company is run. I'm not talking about consumer representatives on the board of management. I'm talking of every member of the board and those at every layer of management, and not only the marketing specialist, seeing himself or herself as a representative of the consumer, being alert to changing needs and committed to meeting them. These people will be consumer representatives first, engineers, accountants or whatever second, or rather, they will use their specialist engineering and accountancy skills as a means of representing the wishes and interests of consumers more efficiently and more comprehensively.

Increasing emphasis on consumer democracy and the technical means of achieving it will require the specialist marketers themselves to be better trained. The body of marketing know-how is increasing year by year and will be required learning for every would-be marketer. The dominance on boards of engineers or the accountants will diminish – and as I've just implied, they'll become much more marketing-oriented themselves. The marketers will take more board level responsibility. After all, it is the marketers who can best guarantee the long-term success of an organisation. In fact I forecast that marketers will head up all the main functions of an organisation, though they may be hybrids – marketer/engineer, marketer/accountant, etc.

Technological developments, some of them not even on the horizon today, will increasingly make the application of consumer democracy very much easier and more foolproof. Companies will be able to manage the detail of their obligations to consumers without, or at least with far fewer of, the embarrassing errors that so often today make a mockery of consumer relationship marketing.

I also forecast that companies will have to take a much broader view of the 'One' in 'All-to-One'. Consumers are far more than merely consumers. Companies will increasingly take on board the fact that the 'One' in 'All-to-One' is not only interested in their products but in a world of other things too, and more interested in them than in any product! These interests can include the environment, Third-World poverty, education, road safety, animal welfare, town planning, everything. It's all very healthy. In fact it's a return to the ideal of the corner store, when the store-owners knew their consumers as friends not as 'consuming units', but as people with names, homes, families and an endless variety of concerns and interests. Enlightened companies are already acting on these lines. Every other will have to follow suit and technology, capable of storing and making accessible any amount and type of consumer information, will empower them.

But I also predict that people, buyers or sellers, will take technology for granted and not allow anything approaching techno-mania to distract them from the only allowable aim of technology and of marketing – to make life better for all concerned. That is an 'All-to-One' future we can look forward to with relish.

Good books to read

T HERE ARE A number of great books on marketing; here are a few words on those I think are the best.

Start your soul-searching here

Loyalty.com: Frederick Newell

Newell's 1997 book, *The New Rules of Marketing*, provoked much soul-searching among the marketing community. In this very readable new book, Lewell sends out the soul-searchers again, this time to find out whether they are going the right way about winning the loyalty of their consumers. It's a kind of Catch 22 situation – the harder you try for loyalty, the less successful you are. The best way, says Newell, is to establish good relations with individuals through all the media but particularly through the Internet. *Loyalty.com* establishes its case with conviction.

Internet changing the world?
It's all happened before

Information Rules: Carl Shapiro and Hal R. Varian

'As the century closed, the world became smaller. The public rapidly gained access to new and dramatically faster communication technologies ... every day brought forth new technological advances to which the old business models seemed no longer to apply. Yet, somehow, the basic laws of economics asserted themselves.' The words are from the brilliant introduction to Shapiro and Varian's book. The century they refer to is the nineteenth century and the technologies that transformed the economy were the 'emerging electricity and telephone networks'. The author's thesis is that 'durable economic principles can guide you in today's frenetic business environment. Technology changes. Economic laws do not'. This is very much a technical 'how to do it' for the e-commerce practitioner, but crisply written and a very good read.

Get courteous – win business

Permission marketing: Seth Godwin

Nothing could be further from the mass-market marketing attitudes of the last century than the philosophy expounded by Seth Godwin in his provocative book. Courtesy is the key to effective marketing – not the kind of statement you used to get in business school. Get the prospect to agree to being approached, and you're well over halfway to the sale and better still to a long-term, high-value relationship with the consumer – or, as Godwin puts it, 'turning strangers into friends and friends into consumers'.

It's a great book which every marketer should read, but I hope Seth won't mind if I point out that his grasp of American history is nothing like as good as his exposition of his brilliant new thesis. Seth likens the impact of the Internet on traditional marketers to the impact of the New World on the feudal lords who, he says, financed the early colonists. Hey, Seth, what about the Pilgrim Fathers and their distinctly non-feudal backers and followers? The USA was built and backed from 1620 onwards by democrats!

How to win in tomorrowland!

Futurize Your Enterprise: David Siegel

This is superb. It's fun, easy to read and full of practical advice and fascinating examples of how and how not to run 'business strategy in the age of the e-consumer'. It's obvious from every page that Siegel is a hands-on practitioner of the gospel he preaches. What especially appeals to me is that he has no time for the Internet hypists. His is a warts-and-all view of the medium, and he shows how to make the very most of its good points (which are legion) and get round the weak ones. I also like Siegel's ability to see through appearance to reality. He points out the dangers of *thinking* that your company is well organised for e-commerce, when in fact the reality is that it is not. Quite a few people in household-name companies might see themselves in some of Siegel's exposés. Nearest to my heart, though, is his emphasis on the consumer and the vital importance of a company being consumer-led. That's the best way to face the future.

Not offensive – rather sophisticated actually

Even More Offensive Marketing: Hugh Davidson

What do you do when you've written a book entitled *Offensive Marketing*? Answer: write a book entitled *Even More Offensive Marketing*. I can't at the moment think of the title of Davidson's next book, but this is enough to be going on with. It's a wonderful guide to life in the marketing department of a multinational FMCG company, with a provocation on every page. I enjoyed relating my own experience to Davidson's charts, diagrams, tables and anecdotes, including those about Virgin. Davidson's legal background shows, perhaps, in his interest in Virgin's technique of competing with much larger organisations with guerrilla tactics, some of them allegedly illegal. Yet Virgin, says Davidson, rarely goes to court, but when it does it usually wins. British Airways could add a gloss to that.

You'll enjoy this book. Apart from the important lessons it has to teach, it gives you endless stories with which to regale your clients over the G&Ts.

A new reformation?

The Cluetrain Manifesto: Rick Levine, Christopher L. Locke, Doc Searls and David Weinberger

This stimulating book began as a website (still there on www.cluetrain.com). The site announced 95 theses, the same number as Luther used to launch the Reformation. The gist of all 95 (the Cluetrain version) is that people are people and markets should be conversations. The advice throughout the book is very sound, very provocative and very usable. It's really about style – the 'how' of communication. It makes the point that a consumer's *perception* is the truth about your company – and the Internet is making the communication of that truth very simple.

Culturequake – are you ready for it?

The New Marketing Manifesto – The 12 Rules for Building Successful Brands in the 21st Century: John Grant

'Culturequake' is the graphic metaphor John Grant uses to brand the re-evaluation of attitudes and beliefs required in the new millennium. Consumers and their culture are changing, and companies must change with them – especially in the way they market their products. His 12 rules show how to do it. They cover everything, including pre-eminently, the need to instil a new consumer-first marketing vision into the entire organisation.

Grant takes a variety of examples to explain his 12 rules and how companies are using them to strengthen their brands. The examples range from multinationals like Coca-Cola and Nike, through to non-corporate brands such as football and The Spice Girls.

The book begins with Grant's definition of 'New Marketing' and his vision of Britain as the home of these new ideas, with examples that include New Labour, Oasis and Damien Hirst.

He discusses each rule in depth (helped by some rather quirky sketches) and ends with 12 case studies of brands which he believes have successfully transformed themselves by using the methods he describes, brands such as BT, French Connection and Labour's New Deal. The book ends with an interestingly ironic look at the old style of marketing and how marketing could be in the future – in a postscript dated 'somewhere in the 21st century'.

'All-to-One' is a journey

HERE'S THE MAP
Every organisation is different! Everyone knows it. Not everyone acts as if they know it. The philosophies and principles I've set out in 'All-to-One' are inevitably generic – they apply to any organisation, but I haven't given you a plan that fits *your* company and *your* brands precisely (you wouldn't expect me to give you that here – your organisation is different from every other. Isn't it?)

You must have a plan of your own, one that connects the needs, aspirations, experiences and mindsets of your market with your own capacities and development capabilities, a plan that links your offering, your positioning, your strengths as an organisation to the positioning of your brands and how you communicate the promise of *those brands to your target markets.*

So ... 'All-to-One' is the overall guiding philosophy ... the RelModel shows you how to develop all the right skills and organisational maturity to exploit your competitive advantage to the maximum. But how do you set about preparing a plan precisely tailored for your company and your brands?

There is any amount of 'plan-making' advice around, but the best I have ever come across and the best in terms of the 'All-to-One' philosophy is the 'Journey Map'. The Journey Map (see back of the book) was created and pioneered by John Caswell, Chief Executive Officer of RMG, which is part of the WPP Group plc (other companies in the Group include J. Walter Thompson, Ogilvy & Mather and Young & Rubicam).

The 'All-to-One' Journey Map is unique, and connects so comprehensively with 'All-to-One' and the RelModel that it is a 'must' for any serious organisation wanting to achieve an answer to the 'What exactly must I do to make 'All-to-One' and the RelModel work for my company?'.

John has been using the Journey Map to advise organisations of many different types and sizes, including the very biggest, in all parts of the world. I have worked with him to develop it in an 'All-to-One' context and create the version included here in the book as a pull-out section.

The map shows you the route at every RelModel level

The essential point is that the 'All-to-One' Journey Map applies to every level of the RelModel. In other words, if you are Level 1, you need to follow the journey laid out in the map. Likewise at Level 2 right through to Level 5. You may do several 'All-to-One' Journey Maps as you climb your way up the RelModel. As each cycle of your marketing operations provides you with better knowledge and closeness to the consumer then you have the ammunition for another 'All-to-One' Journey Map. By following the journey at the level your organisation is at now, you will be far better equipped to move up a level. Then, because of your work at the previous level, you will be able to move along the next level significantly more quickly – and, believe me, more profitably.

The 'All-to-One' Journey Map, as well as showing you the route, also emphasises how the consumer 'DNA', as we put it, must flow through the whole of your organisation, through every department, through every system, organisational process, your product development, your service delivery, your people management, through everyone and everything. Every part of the company and all its activity must be imbued, permeated, utterly influenced by the consumer and the consumer DNA.

This 'All-to-One' Journey Map is a detailed exposition of the Phase 1 of the integrated marketing model described on pages 235–

236. It should be used in conjunction with the model and your marketing operations.

But now, let me now take you through the various parts of the 'All-to-One' Journey Map. It is complex but modular, and so can be broken down into eight major phases.

1. The market focus

At this phase, the focus is on the 'drivers' in the marketplace. These primarily are the motivations and emotions of your consumer – which we call the 'consumer DNA'. The DNA sums up what you have learnt about the individuals that make up your market and their motivations, all of them. The more you learn about the motivations, the better your understanding of the DNA.

This learning process often reveals how much you *don't* know about your consumers. It may even show you what other markets you should be targeting. It will also indicate the RelModel level you are at in terms of understanding the motivations, the DNA, of your target consumers.

At this stage, you will also be identifying competitive activities or any other significant market influences. But the main focus remains on the consumers and their motivations.

2. Consumer targeting and segmentation message matrix

It's a mouthful, but full of nourishment! This is where you start to organise all the fall-out from your evaluation of consumer motivations and define potential segments within your target market. In an ideal world, you would develop a message for each segment, no matter how small. However, economics and other realities dictate that there has to be some 'averaging' so that you end up with an overarching message that appeals to and persuades a larger size of segment. (For example, it is obviously possible to segment households with children into those with children under 10 years and those with children over 10 but under 15. In reality, your message to both segments could be the same and could be in fact completely effective.)

You continue to listen to consumers in each of the segments that interest you and so identify the hierarchy of motivations. By listening, you will be able to develop your products and services in ways that suit the consumers – not the other way round.

You will also be able to identify the right messages, the right tone and the right timing. For instance, the tone you adopt to talk to someone driving to work is different from the tone appropriate to talking to someone driving away on holiday; the way you communicate with someone reading a business magazine at work on a Tuesday morning is different from the way you communicate with someone reading a hobby magazine at home that same evening.

Life-stage analysis at this stage would enable you to understand the differences in usage of your product and the different degrees of receptiveness to your messages by people at different life stages – particularly if your consumer segmentation does not allow for such a level of differentiation. Your messages and their mode of delivery can now be shaped with knowledge of consumer usage of the product and consumer behaviour patterns.

3. Consumer benefits

You can now distil from your analysis a clear list of benefits that the consumer segments would like to see manifested through your products. You need to connect these benefits to consumer motivations via the consumer DNA – which, as I can never overemphasise, connects everything from your product development through to the product delivery and then through to your marketing communications.

4. Channels and partners

Nothing is more critical to your success than your choice of channels and partners, the alliances you set up and the communities you work in – in other words, your routes to the market – via retailer, specialist dealer, value-added reseller, systems integrator, etc. The choice is as important in B2B marketing as it is in consumer marketing. Having made your choice, then the priority is effective and on-going communication. Your channels and partners need supporting and they also need to know your plans and intentions, consumer trends, competitive activity, etc. Newsletters, face to face/ telephone briefing, perhaps an Extranet link, seminars and conferences, certainly regular meetings are all means to the end of efficient and mutually profitable cooperation.

5. Product delivery and service

At this stage you decide how you deliver your promise to the consumer. The key point is that the consumer motivations identified from your earlier analysis must be respected in terms of product delivery and service. In other words, the product must deliver all the promise of the brand as advertised and as experienced in the past. And where applicable, the service that supports it must also be as promised. This means, of course, that all the organisation must continue to focus on the consumer DNA.

Product service, where applicable, is hugely important. Through lack of it, products are often commodities. After all, when manufacturing techniques are so uniformly excellent – take mobile phones as an example – the only differentiator, the only consideration that can build brand status, is service. No service, no brand.

6. Communications optimisation

This is where your messages take their final communicatable shape, providing attractive, persuasive, memorable metaphors of your product and service promises. They must be adaptable for all the chosen media and for all chosen target audiences including the channels and partners. (I have identified all the media now available in Chapter 5). The past saw much misunderstanding at this stage of the journey. People assumed that the people responsible for actually producing the material containing the message – material such as direct mail letters, press ads, TV commercials, etc. – were immune to logic and empirical facts (like what actually motivates potential consumers). The Journey Map makes no such assumption. The same logic and emphasis on facts that direct the rest of the journey are just as significant here, and are ignored at the risk of making the creativity simply cosmetic. The process is continuous. The destination remains the same. The 'consumer DNA' is the guiding thread as much to the creative people as to the research people, and to everybody else. They take their lead, their insights and inspiration from the research – they are driven by it.

7. Marcoms operations

Here is where the marketing communications (Marcoms) are sorted – the packaging, point of sale, communications with channels, promotional activities, consumer advertising, everything is activated. Here as in point 6 above you need to work with an agency which is as holistic in its approach as you are. The days of 'advertising agencies' who didn't know about marketing, or want to know and 'marketing agencies', ditto in reverse, are over. The omnipresent 'consumer DNA' has seen to that.

8. On-going business strategy and product development

This is a finishing-post – or rather the start-again post. When you reach it, you can assess what you have achieved, and consider how to strengthen your strengths and remove any weaknesses. You can now start the journey again – at a higher RelModel level, only this time, as I said before, the journey will be faster and more profitable.

Footnote

There is another wonderful planning process for operational projects, which has been pioneered by Chris Cooper and David Welsh of Challenge Consulting. This particular one delves into your operational priorities connecting with the experience of your consumers and their needs as consumers. I would dearly love to explain this one to you but due to time and space I will leave the detail to another time.

Select glossary

CRM	Consumer relationship marketing (sometimes customer relationship marketing) aims to maximise the lifelong value of the consumer/supplier relationship to both sides.
Cross selling	Selling a bigger variety of products to each consumer/customer.
Consumer champions	People in the company chosen to concentrate on one particular consumer segment and ensure that their interests are fully met in everything the company does.
EPG	Electronically programmed governor – controls who sees what on screen.
Extended virtual network	A group of networks that appears to the user to be one large network.
Information/concierge	People/agency responsible for collecting, keeping, collating and updating information.
MARCOMS	Marketing communications.
Non-consumer dynamics	Influences in the marketplace operating independently of consumers, e.g. the level of advertising expenditure.
Non-real-time information	Information that arrives usually after a short delay, e.g. e-mail, voice mail.

PDA	Personal digital assistant – a hand-held computing device offering basic office services such as e-mail, Internet, word processor.
Real-time information	Information communicated instantaneously between the person sending and the person receiving it, e.g. by voice and video calls and in person.
RelModel	Short for relationship model, a method of maximising supplier/consumer relationships in a controlled and mutually profitable manner.
RelTechnics	Short for relationship techniques – the means whereby the RelModel achieves its objectives.
RelWeb	The RelModel applied to the Internet.
Subsistence marketing	Marketing that aims to achieve only minimal and very short-term targets.
UMPTS	Universal Mobile Phone Telecoms System – third-generation communications standard delivering high-quality video and audio to mobile devices.
Viral	Self-perpetuating/self-multiplying (like a virus). Viral marketing encourages people to talk about a product by presenting its benefits in terms that they enjoy repeating. Viral websites make it easy to forward relevant pages to others. Viral e-mail formats contain promotional messages.
WAP	Wireless application protocol – provides Internet and telephony services on digital mobile phones, pagers, personal digital assistants and other wireless terminals.

Index

R

S

X

Y